ISBN 0-919951-02-3

Copyright © 1982
by
Marcus Books,
195 Randolph Road
Toronto, Canada, M4G 3S6

First printing June 1982.

Cover design by John Roberton.

Manufactured in Canada by Webcom Limited

CONTENTS

INTRODUCTION

Funny, this physical body we humans use... cut it and it bleeds, but then it starts to repair itself from the inside! Exercise it consistently and instead of getting weak it grows stronger! In cases of extreme obesity it can support a weight over 700 pounds, while a six-foot man can weigh under 90 and still function perfectly well. Take it apart and all sorts of oddments come to light. While on the outside it is symmetrical about a mid-plane, inside it's all higglety-pigglety: two lungs, but of different shapes, a heart on the left but none on the right, one stomach off to the side, some 32 feet of hollow rope called intestine, and an appendix that appears to have no use at all aside from keeping a lot of surgeons gainfully employed.

And the bones! Firstly they're on the *inside* (precious little good for protecting us from falls and blows — why not something hard on the *outside* the way a lobster is built? ...now *there's* a life-form for you!) And there's the oddity of having one bone in the top of the leg but two in the bottom ...and all those vertebrae!

But then things go from strange to weird. Someone finds out that by pressing a silver needle into a place on the back, all sensation below the left knee disappears. From somewhere else comes the discovery that the iris is a perfect microcosm of all the important body parts and can be interpreted diagnostically. Reflexology tells us that pressure on the foot can stimulate and cure the internal organs; palmists profess to read the whole course of a life in the configuration of hand lines; and according to phrenology that big lump on your skull is not there just because your older sister clubbed you with a shovel when you were three... it's really a signal that you have artistic talent!

And as if all this weren't enough, Hilarion comes along and tells us that our finger patterns display things from past lives, that every scar, wart and ugly spot has its sorry tale to tell, and that even our individual teeth relate to specific quirks and foibles!

With all this information flashing like neon lights on the body, what is one to do to keep a little privacy? I even heard of at least two fellows who, when they read in *Other Kingdoms* that the marks and creases on the lips accurately time many of the major events of one's life, immediately decided to grown very bushy moustaches!

Jesting aside, it *is* fascinating just how much can be learned about an individual merely by closely observing the structure and markings of the body he inhabits. The purpose of this book is to explain in a cohesive and comprehensive way the patterns of meaning which man's physical body wears – patterns so clear to one versed in the system of interpretation that few secrets remain unrevealed.

Of course, the information in this book is not meant to be used merely for party-time entertainment. The explanations which Hilarion gives in the pages that follow is intended to equip the seeker to help others even more effectively than before – to help them to *know themselves* (a primary goal of incarnation).

For those unfamiliar with the source of this material, Hilarion is the name of an entity whom I am able to contact by using a mind-clearing technique learned from a study of Raja Yoga. He is said in Theosophical writings to be one of the Seven Masters who are responsible for various phases of earth's development. Over the past six years, Hilarion has written some eleven books on various aspects of physical and spiritual reality, all of which are listed on the back cover.

As this is likely to be the last work of any length to be transmitted in the current phase of this channel's activity, I wish to take the opportunity here to express my heartfelt thanks to the many good friends who have pitched in selflessly to make the publication of this series a reality.

To Chris for her tireless efforts, to John for his unwavering support and inspiration, to Larry and Anne for their friendship and work, to Carole who single-handedly produced several of our titles, to Susan W. and John R. for their wonderful covers, to Ruth for all the hours of service, to Art and Joyce for giving us the beautiful *Other Kingdoms*... to all these Light Workers and the many others who have helped with this project, my special appreciation and enduring affection. May your lives be as richly blessed as mine has been through knowing you.

Keep the flame burning.

Maurice B. Cooke
March, 1982
Toronto, Canada

Chapter 1
The Feet

The feet of the human body are rich with significance. Throughout man's development, there have been many indicators pointing to the feet as being of special meaning. For example, when Christ's feet were bathed, there was the intention of conveying servitude, and a humbling of the person doing the washing. Thus, when Christ Himself bathed the feet of the disciples before the Last Supper, He meant to show that He was not above them in any sense, but could carry out the duties of a servant – a graphic illustration of the truth of the saying, that he who would be first must be last.

The feet are planted firmly upon the solid earth. It is through the feet that the body makes its essential contact with the earth plane, and through the muscular control of the feet that balance in the body is maintained. As such, the feet represent that part of the individual which is most closely akin to the material plane of manifestation.

There is a wonderful characteristic regarding the human body which a few individuals suspect, but which is generally not known. It is that virtually every distinct portion of the body is like a microcosm of the body itself – or if not the body, then some other complete level of the individual. Let us illustrate by reminding readers that the study of reflexology attributes to various parts of the foot a direct connection with different portions of the physical body. In the charts used by reflexologists, the major organs of the body are shown either on the

1

sole of the foot or along the two side edges. A typical reflexology diagram is reproduced in Figure 1 of this book.

It is not our purpose here to proceed with a course on reflexology, since there is little that we can add to what is already known by reflexologists who have dedicated themselves to the cure and comfort of their brothers through this wonderful healing technique. Our only comment in regard to this subject relates to the mechanism by which the influences are passed from the foot to the various organs of the body. Within the envelopes of the body are lines of communication which link the different parts together. In the aetheric body, in particular, there are numerous pathways connecting the internal organs with the extremities: the hand, the foot and the ear. The eye is also tied to the internal organs, as well as to the other major body parts, and we shall deal with this wonderful symbolism in detail in the last chapter of the present book. The energies which the reflexologist either awakens within the aetheric body of the patient or adds to the aetheric body from his own, travel along these lines of connection from the foot (or hand) to the corresponding part. By knowing intimately the design of the microcosm on the foot or hand, the practitioner of this excellent healing technique is enabled to direct his curative energy to precisely the part which requires it.

As we have said, it is not our purpose to discourse at length on reflexology. However, there are other areas of symbolic meaning relating to the foot, and these we wish to deal with here.

It is not by accident that the foot of the human being is triangular, as seen from the side. Compare this with the hooves, paws and feet of the animals, which are not triangular in any sense. There is a reason for reserving triangularity to the human foot, and it relates to the true nature of the human being, as compared to that of the various animal species on this planet.

We have pointed out in our earlier books, principally in *Seasons of the Spirit*, that man at the conscious, personality level has three primary facets of his being; these are the mental, the emotional and the physical. Each person has a 'mental life', which involves his activities in studying, reading, talking, writing and thinking. He has also an emotional life, involving all of the emotional and feeling 'hues' which color his life: his affections, his dislikes, his desires, his worries, and so

2

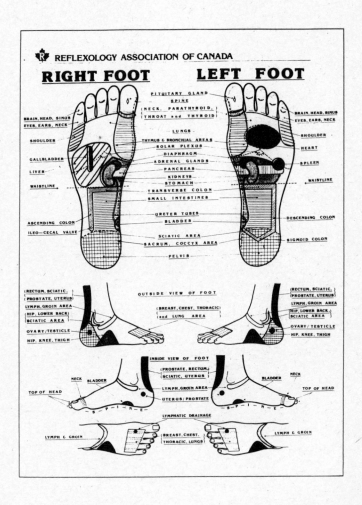

Figure 1

on. Finally he has a physical level of experience, which includes all of the purely physical sensations, whether disagreeable or pleasurable: eating, bathing, athletic activity, making love, and the rest.

In the triangular nature of the foot is found the perfect representation of this 'Triangle of Being' as it has been called. Even the fact that the foot is not an equilateral triangle (one with all sides equal in length) has its significance. The longest 'side' of the foot triangle is that which rests upon the earth: the sole of the foot. This part designates the *physical* side of the individual, and is the longest because it represents the general truth that the physical experience of man is to the fore in importance for most people. This is by no means true of all individuals, but the race as a whole does tend to emphasize the physical pleasures and passions ahead of the purely cerebral experiences and ahead of the 'pure' emotion of love. In accordance with this symbolism, the major internal *physical* organs are found upon the *sole* of the foot in the technique of reflexology.

The arch of the foot is the side of the triangle which is intermediate in length. It represents the mental phase of experience for man, and even though the head centers are not found on the arch, the symbolic meaning nonetheless applies. Indeed, the head and its major organs are located at or just in from the *toes*, which can be considered the *junction* between the sole (physical) and the arch (mental). And this too is perfectly in accordance with our symbolic scheme. For the mental facet of man's experience was intended to allow him to 'lift himself up' from the purely physically-immersed existence of sense and passion, by drawing him away from the ignoble pursuits of pleasure and self into the more rarified areas of mental speculation and study. We have explained in *The Nature of Reality* that the mental adventures were seen, by the guides of humanity, as offering a distinct opportunity to turn the attention of man away from the lower levels of experience, and for this reason various programs of teaching were initiated upon the earth, together with a quickening of the capacity for rational and abstract thought (the latter arising through genetic manipulation and the infusion of superior genetic qualities into the basic 'stock' of the race).

There is thus a further interesting symbology in the foot, relating to the slope of the two triangular 'sides' of the foot thus far discussed. The sole rests flatly against

the earth, i.e. horizontally. This attitude corresponds
to the individual who is drawn only by the physical level
of experience, and suspects nothing of the 'higher' realms
that may await him. The arch of the foot, designating
the mental realm of experience, is at a low angle, but
does reach upwardly to a limited extent. It may be seen
as a first attempt on the part of the individual to lift himself up from the mire of sense and self that makes him
little better than the animals. And yet the arch side of
the triangle does not project straight upwardly; it is
merely 'trying' to raise itself up, and thus represents
only a partial capacity for success. The true access to
the most rarified realms of experience comes through the
emotions, more specifically through the only true emotion,
that of love. We have explained elsewhere that the lesser
emotions of greed, self-pity, hatred, worry and envy are
merely preversions or contortions of the pure love-feeling. The last side of the foot triangle, that of the Achilles tendon (above the heel), represents this possibility
of love for man. It is the shortest of the three sides of
the triangle, and this is meant to convey the fact that,
for most of humanity, the ability to love in the true
sense of the word is as yet only rudimentary.

It is interesting to contemplate the deeper meaning of
the Greek myth of Achilles, in whom the tendon just
above the heel was the weakest and most vulnerable
part of the body. Hence the expression "that is his
Achilles' heel". The love facet of man is indeed that in
which he is the most vulnerable to pain, but principally
because man has not learned to love *freely*. We wish to
say a bit more about this question, because it is so pivotal to living a successful incarnation on the earth plane.

Many individuals have an extremely possessive or an
extremely selfish approach to love and affection. In regard to possessiveness, the tendency to look upon the
'loved one' as property is epidemic. Man is so accustom-
ed to viewing everything about him in proprietary terms
– his car, house, clothes – that he has allowed that distorted view of reality to cloud his affectional life as well.
Many individuals actually regard their spouses as, in
some sense, their personal property. Nothing could be
further from the truth of the matter, and no attitude
could more effectively stand in the way of achieving the
true fullness of love-feeling which human beings were
meant to have for each other.

The essense of love is freedom, and the desire that
the loved one be happy. If the loved one is to be

5

happy, then the lover should want only that which the loved one desires. That is the ideal situation, and if both partners were to adopt it, the relationship would never be in danger of foundering. But too many individuals are afraid to open themselves up to disappointment in this manner. They have in many cases experienced the pain which comes from being taken advantage of by a partner, and they have learned to avoid the openness and commitment that are the prerequisites to the relationship of ideal love which we have described.

But the problem goes deeper. The tendency to view others as merely things or objects has greatly undermined the love relationships which humans establish. If the other is viewed as merely a thing, then there is no possibility of developing the attitude of wanting only that which the other desires. The 'me, mine' approach effectively destroys any chance of two partners dealing with each other as human beings, each with his own worthiness and validity.

Finally, the rampant selfishness which characterises the attitudes of today has fostered the idea that love-partners are for gratification only. There are many forms of such gratification, the sexual being only one, but regardless of the form it takes, the using of another human being merely for self-gratification inevitably degrades the relationship and positively excludes any possibility of developing that true love between equal souls which is the greatest gift that earth existence offers to those in incarnation.

Pride, too, has brought its share of sorrow and aggravation to love-partners on the earth plane. It is chiefly pride that requires a man to be jealous if his wife develops a friendship with another man. It is pride which prompts a woman to badger her husband to improve his financial situation, or dress better, or act in an uncharacteristic way. Cannot individuals love each other *as they are*? If *God* can love each and every one of His earth children with all their foibles and failings, then what right has man to insist that others change? As to jealousy, is it not plain that humans were all meant to love all others, and that love cannot flower fully between two souls when one of them prohibits the other from sending love or affection in another direction?

It may be of interest for readers to realize that one of the main reasons for establishing the *family pattern* among human beings was to teach them to be less stingy and niggardly with their love. Consider what happens:

A man and woman marry, because they have love for
each other. Jealousy and convention require that each
of them focus his love mainly on the mate, and affectional interchange with others is discouraged. But the very
result of their love is to expand the family by bringing
new souls into the earth plane. A baby is born, and
suddenly there is another soul demanding the love and
attention of the two parents. The love-circle now includes three souls and not just the original two. But
the newcomer is small and not in any sense a threat to
either of the parents, so both of them learn to love not
only the partner, but the baby as well. Then another
child comes, then another. Gradually, the love-circle
of the parents is forced wider and wider. What is hoped
from this arrangement is that, ultimately, the parents
will realize that love is not just an exclusive feeling,
but should encompass many other souls as well. If the
parents are spiritually perceptive, they might see finally
that love was intended to be the very glue of the human
race, for without affection as an adhesive, the human
group would shatter and split apart as it is even now
threatening to do.

We wish now to return to the concept of the Triangle
of Being, for we have here an opportunity to illustrate
it graphically, whereas in our earlier writings this was
not convenient.

The human being combines three distinct levels of experience: the mental, the emotional and the physical.
This can be represented as in Figure 2, where the sides
of the triangle have been appropriately labeled. The
figure there drawn has equal sides, symbolizing the ideal
situation in which the individual has developed these
three areas of experience equally, and has not allowed

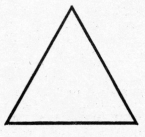

Figure 2

one to dominate the others and force them into the back-
ground. Examples of such lop-sided persons are easy to
find in the world today: the college professor whose entire world is that of the mind, and who has neglected
both his physical body and his emotional life in order to
push his intellect to the very limits of understanding; or
again, the weight-lifter who is utterly obsessed with the
beauty or strength of his physical vehicle, and has
never cared to develop his understanding or allow his
affectional nature to expand; or lastly, the person who
is totally at the mercy of his emotions, constantly swept
away on a tide of feeling that his mind cannot control.
All of these are examples of off-center development of
the Triangle of Being, and for each, it will be necessary
to redress the imbalances that have been allowed to develop, in order to bring the *lower* triangle into equilibrium
along with the *upper* triangle. We have here introduced
the notion of two triangles, and although we have dealt
with the concept of higher self and lower self in our
earlier writings, we consider that the discussion is
worth following through again, with the aid of the dia-
grams which this book contains.

Man is not merely his everyday personality. Indeed,
the Romans understood this fact when they used the
word 'persona' to designate the mask worn by actors in
plays. It is from that Latin root that the word 'personality' is derived, and here we have the representation of
an important truth, namely that the *personality* of an
individual is merely a 'mask' which the individual assumes
for the duration of a specific life, and which is set aside
after the life is over.

It is this personality which we call the *lower self*. It
has its own triangle of being, the lower triangle, and it
is this which incarnated individuals manifest to each
other. It is important to realize that a lopsidedness in
the lower triangle does not necessarily correspond to a
similar lopsidedness in the *higher self* or soul, although
in many cases this does occur. Let us use two examples
to illustrate our meaning.

Consider a personality who is very much at the mercy
of his emotions, and who allows his feelings and moods
to control his life pattern, to get him into arguments
with others, and to lead to long stretches of depression
and ill-health. Now, this 'package' of traits which the
lower self is manifesting can, in the first case, represent almost exactly a similar lopsidedness in the higher
self. In such an instance, the purpose of the life pat-

tern would be to allow these higher self traits to manifest in the same lopsided way in the earth personality, so that they can draw the personality into difficult situations, sorrow and heartbreak – precisely so that the lower self will ultimately realize that *it is these inner traits that are responsible for the difficulties.* For if this realization can be attained, then the same truth can dawn upon the higher self, and through effort some rebalancing of the lopsidedness can be achieved.

In the other case, the higher self may be quite balanced, but for special reasons it may decide to project a lopsided personality. The reasons can relate to the path chosen by the soul, or perhaps the soul wishes to test its grasp of truth by deliberately causing its perceptions to be masked to some extent. Let us give instances of these two cases.

Suppose a soul has volunteered for a *sacrifice life.* This term designates a life in which the soul wishes to play some role of broad significance to humanity as a whole. For example, a soul may be asked to consider living in circumstances in which it is possible that it will rise to the presidency of the United States. If it agrees, then certain special characteristics must, in most cases, be 'overlaid' on the personality to allow it to attain this position. To begin with, we must emphasize that most who attain or who nearly attain that particular station in life are quite advanced souls. That level of responsibility cannot be given to a soul of unevolved status, because too much depends upon the actions which the personality takes. Now such evolved souls, at the higher levels, normally do not have the ego and worldly drive necessary to make it to that high office. Moreover, most such souls would be incapable of the sort of compromise of principles which any presidential candidate must accede to in order to secure the nomination of his party. Therefore, an overlay must be given to the personality which will contribute to the individual the ambition, ego and willingness to 'make deals' that the presidency requires. Without that overlay, he would shy away from politics, and never enter the ring.

But how are these characteristics applied? Mainly it is done through the astrological timing of the birth, together with a selection of parents which will fan the embers of ego and worldly ambition that the astrological influences impart. Some contribution can come genetically as well, but this is a minor factor.

Another point should be made in regard to such sacrifice lives. This relates to an agreement on the part of the entering soul to allow the physical body to be damaged or killed, if the guides of humanity decide that such is best for the advancement of the race spiritually. Kennedy had given his assent to this possibility prior to his birth, although it was not known at that time that he would definitely become president in 1960. However, when he did gain the presidency, the guides decided, for a number of reasons, that it would be appropriate for him to be taken out of earth existence in the manner which occurred. Most of those in high office have made the same commitment, and this applies also to many others in the public eye. John Lennon was an example.

Turning to the other case, that in which the soul wishes to test its grasp of truth or its ability to make the right choices, we may describe a soul who wishes to put itself through the temptation of sexuality, in which it must decide to what extent the sexual side of experience will influence its affectional and physical actions. However, suppose that the soul is very nearly in balance in terms of this lesson. If there is a near balance, then the mere projection of a personality will not guarantee that the lopsidedness will arise. And yet the soul *wishes* to be born with such an imbalance, in order to make the test as rigorous as possible. In other words, the soul wants to be sure that, even in adverse conditions, it will have the inner perception to be able to discern the truth, and make the right decisions.

Again, the only way by which this sexual overemphasis can be superimposed on an essentially balanced soul is through astrologically timing the birth so that the right planetary factors will be present. For example, by timing the birth with Mars in Scorpio or Capricorn, or with Mars in the eighth house, the necessary lopsidedness can be effected.

We wish now to return to our discussion of the two triangles: the higher and the lower. In Figure 3 there are illustrated two triangles to represent these concepts. The upper triangle has its apex pointing upwardly to represent the idea that the higher self maintains its attention primarily on the 'higher' values, the truths of the spirit, etc. By contrast, the lower triangle has its apex pointing downwardly, signifying that the lower self or personality finds its attention drawn inevitably downwardly into practical considerations, day-to-day concerns, and the realities of earthly life in a physical body.

Now, according to the Mysteries, one goal of earth incarnation is to bring the higher and lower selves as close together as possible, so that the experience and practical knowledge of the lower is available to the higher, and so that the wisdom and spirituality of the higher is infused into the lower. This ideal state of affairs is represented by drawing the two triangles directly over one another, as is illustrated in Figure 4. Readers will be surprised to recognize in this figure one of the most ancient and holy of all symbols given to man. Yet it is far more than merely the Star of David. It was a part of the spiritual heritage of humanity long before the Jewish race had its beginning. And so long as man continues to manifest himself on the lower planes of crea-

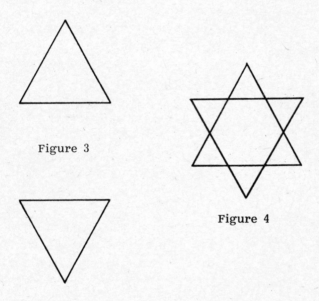

Figure 3

Figure 4

tion, this lovely symbol — reflected back to him a billion-fold in every snowfall — will keep itself before his inner eye.

In the next chapter we will move on to the leg as a symbol of the desired alignment of the higher with the lower self.

Chapter 2
The Leg

The symbolic meaning of the human leg is one that few occultists are aware of. It was intended as a constant reminder of a major goal of earth incarnation, namely to bring the lower self into alignment with the higher self. To this end, the lower part of the leg denotes the lower self, while the upper part – the thigh – represents the higher self or soul.

The symbolic meaning for the lower portion of the leg, the calf, is tied to the fact that the lower leg has *two* bones in it, compared with the single bone in the upper part.

The lower self, as it manifests on the earth plane, typically includes both male and female characteristics. Usually, the higher self will allow the traits which partake of the sexual identity of the body to be to the fore, and to manifest more strongly. At the same time, the traits which belong to the sex opposite that of the body will be more hidden and suppressed.

It is important to understand that the higher self – the soul – does not have a sexuality as such, at least not to the same degree as is found upon the earth. The higher self generally possesses a more balanced mixture of male and female traits, even though in general a given soul would be found to lean somewhat more to one sexual category than to the other. When a soul projects a selection of its characteristics down into earth manifestation, it may choose to do so in either sexual identity in terms of the physical body. When it manifests as female on the earth plane, it draws mainly upon its female side to form the outer personality. However, there will always be some flavor of the male side as well, these masculine tendencies being largely present in the subconscious and only partially manifesting through the conscious personality. The degree of suppression of the traits belonging to the opposite sex depends upon a number of factors, among them the family attitudes, cultural pressures, and the genetically inherited drives and tendencies of the body itself.

Conversely, a soul that projects into a male body will normally select mainly the masculine characteristics of itself for conscious manifestation, including some female traits as well – at either the subconscious or conscious levels.

Now, the presence of a dominant sexual identity and a hidden sexual identity exactly corresponds to the position and relative prominence of the two bones in the lower leg. Taking a female personality as an example, the composite of female traits which make up the conscious self is represented by the bone that is toward the front in the lower leg. This is called the shin bone or tibia. It is this bone that takes the brunt of any blow on that part of the anatomy, and it is the one that can be easily felt by the hand along its whole length. Conversely, the fibula – the second bone of the lower leg – is smaller than the tibia, and generally is covered up by the calf muscle, so that it cannot easily be felt with the hand except near its extremities. The 'hidden' position of the fibula denotes the hidden or suppressed nature of the opposite-sex characteristics of the lower self. In our example of the female personality, the fibula then represents the male side.

The relative availability of these two bones, i.e. the ease with which they can be felt by the hand, represents in a general way the relative weights of the two sexual sides in the personality. Hence those with very little calf muscle, and whose fibula is easily felt, will generally demonstrate a more equal mix of male and female traits. This is not to say that the presence of both sides will detract necessarily from the physical appearance. An example of the working out of this process would be the female who is very feminine in appearance and certain mannerisms (the female side, as represented by the tibia), but who has strong drives to succeed in business or a career (the male side – fibula). It is safe to assume that persons who have noticeably thin calves probably have chosen to manifest some prominent trait of the opposite sex in this life pattern.

When any damage, accident or illness occurs in one of the two lower leg bones, there is a 90% likelihood that the person's guides are using the incident as a way of reminding the individual – at the subconscious level – that some key concept relating to one of the sexual 'halves' is being highlighted, needs to be thought about, or whatever. For example, a child around the age of puberty may damage one or both of these bones in an accident. The particular bone damaged will be an indicator that some aspect of that side of the sexual picture is requiring effort or a learning process. The possibilities in terms of specific lessons are very broad, and we cannot set down a hard and fast rule to use in all such cases. However, we are confident that the seeker, equipped with the foregoing explanation, will be able to use his own intuition and reasoning ability to arrive at the correct interpretation.

Turning now to the upper leg or thigh, it is well known that this part of the leg contains only a single bone, the femur. The femur is the longest and strongest of all the bones in the human body, and must be so in order to handle the mechanical loading that is placed upon it during strenuous sports.

The femur represents the higher self or soul. The fact that there is but a single bone in the upper leg denotes the fact that the soul is, in general, far more unitary than the personality in terms of sexual characteristics. The soul level is that on which all traits of both sexes – to the extent that the soul has acquired these – manifest freely.

The femur can be damaged or can develop certain kinds of diseases which impair its function. To explain the symbolic nature of these indicators, we first must point out the significance of the knee and the hip – the anatomical parts at either end of the femur.

The knee is literally the joining link between the femur and the bones of the lower leg. As such, it represents the connection or link between the higher and the lower selves. If the knee is weak or subject to disease, it is signalling that the communication between the personality and the soul is weak or very rudimentary. Usually this occurs to a person who has allowed the attractions of the world to sway him away from any interest in higher spiritual things. A person for whom material possessions are everything, or who thinks only of sex,

15

or the self, or money, is one to whom such a reminder
might be given.

When the knee becomes so debilitated that there is a
danger that the knee cap may have to be amputated,
the individual is at a critical phase in his development
on the earth plane. Unless he or she makes a special
effort to re-establish contact with the higher self or
soul, there is a danger that the personality, after
death, will not be able to rejoin the higher self and will
become lost in the lower astral worlds. If this happens,
then the soul may never be able to re-assimilate its projected personality, and as a result the soul will lose a
part of its essence permanently.

Turning to the hip joint, this is constituted by a soc-
ket in the hip bone – the acetabulum – into which the
head of the femur fits. The joint is a universal one, allowing the femur to swivel to many directions and not
limiting motion only to a given plane. The fact that the
joint is universal represents the *freedom* which the soul
or higher self is given by the creative forces to forge
its own path through the planes of reality. Man has free
will, and though he is expected to learn to harness that
freedom into the service of creation and love, he is nonetheless allowed the perfect right to travel in any direction he chooses, on the understanding that he must always 'pay his dues' under the karmic law of cause and
effect.

In view of the foregoing, it will be understood that
the hip bone (pelvis) represents the creative forces
which have made humanity and have set it free to find
its own way through reality. Being 'creative' in its
symbolic meaning, it is natural that this part of the body
should house the most creative, i.e. the *pro-creative*,
organs. Hence, in a sense, the pelvis represents the
creative powers or God – at least for the *leg* symbology.
(However, diseases of the hip bone *per se* have a different level of meaning which we will deal with in a later
chapter.)

Turning again to the femur, it will be grasped that the
meaning of any disease or break in the femur is dependent upon the *location* of the femur which is involved.
A disease of the femur head, for example, will point to
the link between the soul and the higher planes beyond
it, from which it draws sustenance. Any such disease
or break will suggest that the higher self must learn to
integrate itself more into creation, and this can be accomplished by doing the same at the lower self level. In

other words, the lower personality has only one possibility of influencing the higher self or soul, and that is to work on *itself*. For any changes which take place in the lower self automatically are reflected in the higher self. Thus one who has a problem of any kind at the upper end of the femur should turn his attention toward the higher truths and the cosmic laws, for if these can be assimilated at the conscious level, they will automatically become a part of the soul.

If the disease or break is at or close to the knee, the signal likely is that the soul's ability to communicate with the lower personality is impaired in some way. This may be a flaw in the soul (most likely), although it could also be the fault of the conscious personality. Effort will have to be expended in re-establishing the faltering communication between the lower and the higher parts of the individual.

Finally, the most intriguing symbol of all regarding the leg is that of straightening it out. To straighten the leg from a bent condition involves bringing the upper into *alignment* with the lower part. The meaning is, of course, to bring the higher self into alignment with the lower or conscious personality. It is precisely the same message that is offered by the six-pointed star which we discussed in the first chapter of this book.

A last word is in order about the act of kneeling, as when praying. The act of kneeling has always represented the subjugation of one's will to that of another, whether to a king or to God. By bringing the lower end of the femur into contact with the ground in the act of kneeling, the individual is literally making contact between the earth and that part of his anatomy which designates the link between his lower and higher selves. This represents the most significant part of his soul-structure, for without this link nothing of value can be learned from an earth incarnation. By touching the earth itself with the symbol of the higher/lower link, one is symbolically stating the importance of the link with respect to earth life. By assuming this position in prayer, the ego, the subconscious and the higher self are all reminded that the goal of material incarnation is to weld the higher and lower together, and that God's help is needed in the task.

In the next chapter we will turn our attention to the symbology of the left and right sides of the body.

Left Side, Right Side

The symbolism of the left and right sides of the body
is simple to explain, but often requires considerable in-
sight to interpret in a manner that will have significance
for the person for whom this means of message-passing
is used.

Generally speaking, the left side of the body refers
to the 'package' of female characteristics and traits
which are present in the lower personality. The right
side, conversely, denotes the male tendencies and characteristics. Hence, a problem arising on the left side
of the body, in addition to having a meaning in terms of
the particular part affected, will also normally have some
significance relating to the *side* of the body involved.

Let us use an example out of the last chapter. In that
part of the book, we dealt with the symbolism of the leg
per se, independently of *which* leg is involved. Let us
assume that a boy of 13 has a skiing accident in which
the left tibia and the right fibula are damaged or broken
in some manner. Now, the tibia for a boy will denote the
male traits which he is manifesting at the conscious personality level. However, the injured tibia is on the *left*
side, and therefore the accident is also saying something
about the female portion of his total self. The damaged
fibula denotes the female traits for him, but is on the
right, therefore suggesting something to do with the
male characteristics. The question, then, is how to interpret this confusing set of indicators. The approach is
always the same: isolate the factors, and deal with them
separately. *Then* attempt a synthesis. Taking first the
injured left tibia, we would assume that the *bone* is the

dominant indicator, thus pointing directly to something
relating to the male side of the personality. This could
be some normally male tendency which is being neglected,
or which is being over-emphasized in an unbalanced way.
The matter would have to be judged on the basis of the
actual person involved. Often the sensitive interpreter
will, because of his familiarity with the person afflicted,
be able to spot immediately the area designated by the
injury. As to the fact that the injury occurs on the
left side, normally associated with the female area in
some way, again the interpreter would have to look to
his intuition for the answer, based upon his knowledge
of the life circumstances and traits of the subject. For
example, the over-emphasis of male traits (tibia) could
be interfering with his relationship with the principle representative of female qualities, his mother. Many
other possibilities are also available.

The fibula on the left side would refer to female traits
in the first instance, but with some associated problem
pertaining to the male side. Perhaps the boy is neglect-
ing or strenuously suppressing certain female parts of
himself, such as his kindness to animals or his sympathe-
tic nature, and as a result is running into problems connected with the male side. For example, his suppression
of the female side may be unbalancing his sexual development and leading to excessive masturbation or nocturnal
emission experiences. As can be seen, the problems are
often of a very personal nature, and it is not the case
that individuals afflicted in these symbolic ways will always be ready to talk freely about the possible areas of
significance. As with everything which pertains to analysis and occult interpretation, the best subject for study
is oneself. Ultimately, these signals and clues are meant
to be understood directly by the person to whom they
occur. Indeed, this always happens at the subconscious
or super-conscious (higher self) level, whether or not
the conscious personality is also able to comprehend
what is being pointed out.

Other instances of right/left symbolism are often easier to interpret. For example, when the femur on one
side is diseased or damaged, then the message pertains
to the part of the *higher self* that includes the appropriate sexual characteristics. The right femur will be
the male package of traits as these manifest at the higher
level, while the left femur will denote the female.

Having now dealt with the leg, we wish to turn to the
major organs in the trunk of the human body.

Chapter 4
The Major Organs and Systems

There is a general understanding among those interested in hidden symbolism that the major parts of the body are directly related to various kinds of problems, tendencies and lop-sided behavior. Most occultists, for example, will appreciate readily that someone who has a weak or damaged heart must learn something having to do with love. This is not to say that the person is not capable of loving. In many cases, the problem is not how to love, but how to love *everyone*. Love is not a true spiritual emotion when the individual at the same time harbors dislike or hatred for some other person. To love someone truly requires that hatred and resentment be erased from one's emotional experience, for otherwise the love is weakened and conditional. It is not true, as some think, that one's love is intensified by the fact that an equally intense dislike is held for some third person. There is a false notion abroad that a maximum love experience can only be had by one who feels *all* emotions with great intensity, including the negative emotions like hatred. This is an illusion. The Christ Love experience — the greatest available to man on the earth — can only be had by one who has eradicated from his heart the last vestige of negativity, resentment and dislike. The Love which the Christ came to demonstrate to mankind cannot co-exist with any emotion that separates human beings from one another.

Let us begin this discussion with the organs and systems which are located toward the bottom of the trunk of the human body, and gradually work up toward the top.

The Reproductive System

The system which the human body employs to continue the race through reproduction is one of the most wonderful and 'occult' systems in the physical vehicle of man. We use the word 'occult' because there are certain functions and processes forming a part of the reproductive cycle which operate in a way that is quite misunderstood by science. Indeed, there are some processes that require intervention from higher planes and other dimensions in order to operate properly. We wish to explain some of these processes in this chapter.

When a male and a female engage in sexual intercourse, there are many interchanges of energy and substance which take place at levels other than the physical. In addition to the implantation of the male sperm in the birth canal of the female, there is a sharing of the root-chakra energies of the two partners in such a way that the void or lack of male energy in the female and of female energy in the male is compensated. We stress that this interchange of root chakra energy between the partners can only take place between two who care for each other at levels beyond and above the purely physical one of passion and chemical attraction. Those who are promiscuous by nature, and who refuse to allow themselves to become emotionally attached to those with whom they have sexual experience, are guaranteeing that no balancing of the root chakra energy will take place during the act of intercourse.

Other hidden processes occur as well. In order for a female egg to be penetrated by a male sperm in a way that will allow an *advanced* soul to enter the foetus after its formation, there *must* be some form of love or affection between the two partners *at the time of the orgasm which led to the conception.* The love or caring is essential, for it surrounds the forming embryo with a protective envelope at a finer vibration than the physical, one which is necessary for all evolved souls for it shields them against the negative influences coming from the earth plane during the nine months of gestation. Now, many children are conceived between partners who do not care for each other and who have no emotional attachment to bind them together. In such cases, the embryo can only be inhabited by a soul whose basic vibrational rate is no higher than that of the material plane itself — a generally unevolved being — and it is in this way that so many of the criminals, murderers and anti-social individuals have gained access to the earth.

Now, having explained the essential component for allowing an evolved soul into the world, we have also explained the most appropriate attitude to take toward the whole sexual experience, i.e. one which represents having *learned the sexual lesson at the material level of experience.* For it is the failure to learn the sexual lesson which leads to all diseases, infirmities and malfunctions of the reproductive tract, whether congenital or not. We wish to explain this matter in greater detail.

There are many 'unevolved' attitudes in the world today in regard to the subject of sex. Some view the matter in strictly selfish terms. They wish merely to obtain self-gratification through the sex act, and they are incapable of any warmth, caring or even gratitude toward the partner. Such individuals are found often among men who frequent brothels, where they hire the body of a woman solely to attain sexual release. Unfortunately, the release is always and only at the physical level, and no interchange of root chakra energy can possibly be accomplished between the partners. As a result, the release is only partial, and the continually building root chakra imbalance (i.e. the continual storage of more and more male-side root chakra energy) will propel the victim into further such episodes. He will think that he has a strong 'sex drive', but will not realize that the drive is the result of his imbalance, and is not due to any physical prowess on his part. The same phenomenon occurs in those who frequently masturbate. Masturbation merely releases the *physical* pressures, and cannot interchange root chakra energy since the partner is lacking. A vicious circle of ever more frequent masturbation is very common in both men and women who allow the cycle to start.

Many seekers have wondered whether any karma attaches to the act of masturbation, and we wish to explain the matter here. Basically, the word karma means cause-and-effect. Thus, any effect resulting from a cause can be looked on as in conformity with the law of karma. Now, masturbation entails an imbalance of root chakra energy which is never released and therefore continually builds up, urging the victim into ever more frequent masturbatory episodes. *That* is the 'karma' associated with the act of masturbation. There is no karma carried over into future lives because the effect arising in the same life as the act itself is quite appropriate in terms of negative result.

Turning again to the lopsided views of sex, there is

one which in particular is responsible for much emotional
suffering in the world. That is the attitude which sees
the partner as merely a 'love-object' to be *made love to,*
but whose own pleasure or happiness are not the concern
of the lover. Let us be more specific. There are men
who fancy that they love a woman intensely. These men
wish to have sexual intercourse with their partners because they see sex as a way to demonstrate their love,
and because they have strong sex drives in any event.
However, it never crosses their mind that the essence
of a true love feeling is *consideration* for the other person. As such, these men fail to satisfy their women,
and indeed never concern themselves with whether the
women are happy or not. They are wrapped up so much
in their own emotional experience that they forget that
the partner is also a human being with her own needs
and desires. This situation shows another face of selfishness even though the partner guilty of this kind of
behavior would strenuously deny that he/she were being
selfish. They would justify their attitudes or actions on
the basis of their 'deep love'.

Finally, there is an enormously damaging attitude on
the part of many persons, that sex is somehow 'dirty'
or debasing. Such people view sex as a necessary evil,
one to be tolerated only in strictly defined circumstances
and justifiable only for procreative purposes. This cor-
rosive point of view has embittered many otherwise noble
souls against certain of the most beautiful aspects of
earth experience, because in rejecting the sexual experience as degrading they are turning their backs on one
of the greatest gifts which the Father has offered for
the comfort, solace and pleasure of His earth children.
And to turn one's back on God's gifts is to reject the
true meaning of existence and to invite sorrow, bitterness and loneliness into one's life.

To summarize, then, the presence of any abnormality,
illness, disease or malfunction of the reproductive system *always* points to a lesson yet to be learned in connection with the matter of sex. Even the inherent weaknesses or predispositions which are only triggered by
foreign substances – such as gels, creams or other forms
of contraception – must be considered to be a pointer or
a reminder. In the case of congenital problems in the
reproductive area, the damage is always karmic in nature. Often this arises due to the failure of the soul
properly to form the related body parts, because of its
own imbalance in that area.

The Renal System

The renal system is one of the major means which the body uses to rid itself of poisons, toxins and wastes. As such, the symbolic meaning of the renal system is that of *expressing externally that which is within*. Those who will not allow their natural inclinations to surface, who repress any quality, tendency, desire, ability or belief, automatically predispose their renal systems to illness and malfunction. This system is vibrationally akin to the process which the self uses to express and move to the outside that which it harbors within.

The thing repressed and not allowed to surface is not always something negative. There are cases in which a soul is not permitting *spiritual knowledge or abilities* to be expressed, and where the result is serious kidney malfunction, weakness and disease. The man who suppresses criticism of his wife's drinking habits; the woman who, through fear of criticism, quashes her strong desire to push hard in her career; the child who, to please his parents, denies certain strong inborn traits which he has – all of these are candidates for renal problems.

One might well ask, is not the suppression of a negative trait a good thing? For example, why should someone who is holding criticism in check be 'punished' by kidney difficulties? The answer is simple. Remember always that man makes his own illnesses for himself. No physical problem is decreed as a punishment. Remember too that the body has certain natural functions and processes, and that physical existence at the material level *must* conform to the laws of the plane of matter in order to avoid difficulties. One of these laws is that of self-expression. Man descends into physical matter in order to learn about himself. If he refuses to allow out that which is within, how is he ever to learn what he is really like? The law thus calls for expression of the internal essence. We have explained elsewhere that the function of earth life is such that one's entire *environment* takes up and reflects back the essential traits that are within. He who harbors hatred and resentment will live a life of agitation, friction and harassment. He who allows only love and kindness to reside within him, will draw to him only those persons and things which are harmonious and pleasant.

Turning to the particular case which began this discussion, we think many seekers will realize instinctively that merely *suppressing* criticism is not the answer.

The true solution is *not to have the criticism inside at all*. The individual who does not allow a single critical thought to cloud his mind has truly learned the lesson.

The Digestive System

The digestive system includes a number of distinct parts.

Let us first discuss the stomach, since this is the principle organ of digestion. In the stomach the main work of breaking down food into its different components takes place. And here too, the food is prepared for assimilation. Some assimilation occurs directly through the stomach walls, while other phases must take place through the intestinal walls.

The meaning of the stomach, in spiritual and symbolic terms, is that of digesting and assimilating experience. The stomach signifies the part of the individual that can learn the lessons which are held out constantly by reality, and which is able to accept that which is taught. Many people resent others to such an extent that the ability to learn lessons in an incarnational experience is impaired. The resentment clouds the inner perception and as a result little improvement is made during the life-pattern in the earth plane. Because resentment, bitterness and dislike are the principle blocks to assimilation of the lessons which earth life was meant to teach, it often happens that stomach illness intervenes for one who has allowed these traits to invade him. Ulcers are the principle manifestation of resentment, in the present phase of earth experience. However, any form of indigestion, distension or gas must be looked on as possibly signifying something akin to resentment. In certain cases, the tendency responsible for the gastric problem is not resentment per se, but rather an agitation and tenseness due to the pace of life, the demands which a busy existence makes, and the multiple expectations of others. All such harassment tends to interfere with the quietness of mind which is necessary to allow the introspection that alone can lead to a full grasp of one's life-lessons.

Thus, even though the immediate cause of gastric difficulties is often tension, worry, resentment and the like, the *true* reason why these inner traits lead to stomach problems is that they interfere with the main goal of life: to learn that which improves the soul, to master the lessons for which earth life was undertaken.

The intestinal areas can be looked on as an extension of the assimilative functions of the stomach. Since the intestines too are principally involved with the assimilation of food, it stands to reason that illness and malfunction in these areas likewise points to a failure to learn the lessons of life from a spiritual point of view.

A final word, however, is in order with regard to the ravages which the current North American diet causes to the digestive system. The rampant increase in cancer of the colon is directly the result of heavy meat-eating, particularly red meat. This connection is now known to conventional medical science, and it is a stark comment on the refusal of humanity to give up its self-indulgences that even this proven correlation has not significantly lowered the eating of animal cadavers.

Naturally, the colonic cancer victim is also being shown something else through his disease: namely that his basic ability to learn and assimilate the lessons of his life-pattern is very poor. The fact that he has developed colonic rather than stomach cancer, for example, is due in most cases to the fact that he was a heavy red-meat eater prior to the onset of the cancer.

Further on this point, we have said elsewhere that cancer is always given in cases where fundamental life-lessons have not been learned to the point of 50%, as judged by the guides of the soul concerned. In the case of one who has closed down his learning apparatus, who listens not to the advice or counsel of others, who believes that he himself knows it all and needs no other guide, the disease of cancer is always considered as a means to jolt the individual into an awareness of his shortcoming. Since the lack is in the area of assimilation, naturally the digestive tract is the most appropriate to be attacked. The only question is, which part of the tract should be selected? The matter is judged on the basis of which part is weakest at the time of inspection. Some have weak colons genetically. Others predispose the colon to illness through a heavy diet of meat. In others, it is the stomach which is the weakest, due to the harboring of resentment and dislike. We are attempting to show here that the conventional view that diet predisposes certain organs to cancer is compatible with the idea of cancer as an essentially spiritual disease — one given to bring home in stark terms a realization of the areas where the soul must strive to make improvement.

The Digestive System also includes certain other organs which contribute importantly to digestion.

The Pancreas

The first of these ancillary organs to be discussed here is the pancreas. The pancreas has a number of functions, but one of the most important is that of allowing the body to balance the sugar level in the blood. With the great availability of sweets in the earth today, the pancreas has been called upon to secrete far more insulin than was the case in past ages when sugar was not so readily available in the refined state. We wish to discuss sugar in this book, because few are aware of the ravages to which they subject their bodies through the ingesting of refined sugar in any form.

It is the case that man *was* meant to have sugar as a part of his dietary intake. However, the wise shepherds of the race – those who designed the physical vehicle and provided the means in nature by which it could be sustained – did not intend that man should debase natural forms of sugar by refinement. The carbohydrates which man can find in nature basically include fruit sugars and starchy vegetables. In the latter category are potatoes, yams, bananas, beets, grains and other sources. The digestive system which man was given is ideally suited to absorb properly these natural materials, whether in the raw or the cooked state. Of course, most foods for man are best eaten in the raw state, although some – notably the potatoe – are preferable after cooking lightly to convert some of the components which would otherwise be unassimilable.

When the human body takes in a whole fruit, it does ingest the sugar which the fruit contains. This was planned. However, the fruit contains much more than merely the sugar. It contains numerous enzymes, minerals and other factors at the physical, astral and aetheric levels which contribute importantly to the task of digesting the sugar. Without these additional materials, the digestive system is literally not able to digest the sugar content in a healthy way. Thus, when man strips away these additional factors, for example through the refining of the sugar cane, the refined sugar which results is not something for which the human body was designed, and its ingestion can only be harmful. Naturally it is a question of quantity. Small portions of candy or the like made with refined sugar will only cause marginal damage, but the average North American eats far too much of this dangerous material, and has caused serious ravages in his system by the time he

28

reaches age thirty.

One of the most grievously damaged parts of his body is the pancreas. Because of the inordinately high sugar intake, the pancreas has had to overwork for years, and in many people this produces a weakening of its ability to perform its function. For some, the result is a chronic *over-secretion* of insulin, leading to cases of low blood sugar, or hypoglycemia. In most such cases, the person has over-indulged in sweets in a previous life, and the result is a congentially weak pancreas in the present physical body.

In other cases, the pancreas simply gives up, and cannot any longer secrete sufficient (or any) insulin. Diabetes is the result. Again, the illness is usually prepared in a previous life of over-indulgence in sweets.

This brings us directly to the symbolic meaning of the pancreas per se. It is that of over-indulgence or self-indulgence. But the meaning is not restricted to food. In other words, he who has a problem with his pancreas may be self-indulging in emotional excess, or in violence or in any of the other areas of negative self-expression, and this may be at the root of pancreatic illness or malfunction. The seeker who wishes to get to the bottom of any case where the pancreas is inadequate or diseased will have to become familiar with the whole lifepattern of the victim.

The Liver

This organ is that which corresponds to the idea of balance, equilibrium and 'normalcy'. In many ways, it represents the concept of 'good sense' and sanity in terms of the higher self. We should point out, in connection with sanity, that for the higher self there is no such thing as mental illness. Mental illness is normally defined as a certain inability to cope with the requirements of a normal productive life. Those who suffer in the mind are usually unable – to a greater or lesser degree – to 'manage' the details of their lives properly. A certain lack of the sense of reality is also a part of many mental imbalances, in the sense that the victim is not able to distinguish that which arises from within his mind from that which has an objective reality apart from the observer. We do not wish to enter into a philosophical discussion as to what constitutes 'objective reality'. It is enough to point out that there is a general concensus as to what constitutes the normal objective world, and that those afflicted in the mind often do not share that concensus.

29

We have said that in the higher self, there is no mental illness. This affliction arises only in the earth personality, and is almost always due to a mismatch between the mental nature of the lower self and that of the higher self. When the divergence becomes too great, the energies of the higher self cannot enter the lower personality to support mental activity at the earth level, and as a result the capacity for rational perception and sane judgement becomes impaired.

It should be pointed out that, in many cases diagnosed as mental aberration, the cause is also *chemically* related. Because of the mismatch between the higher mind and the lower minds that have been projected in past incarnations, it sometimes happens that the soul (higher self) is not able to properly form the brain of the foetus while it is in the womb. When this occurs, a hormonal or chemical imbalance arises, and it is this which places the extra pressures on the lower mind – indeed, it is this which, in large part, stands in the way of a full and proper communication between the higher and lower minds of the individual.

We have digressed into the question of mental illness for an important reason, namely to explain that at the higher self level no one is ever mentally ill. Having said this, however, it remains true that some higher minds of certain individuals, while not irrational, are nonetheless quite lopsided in their emphasis – so much so that when it comes time for that higher self to project another earth personality, the body itself, and specifically the *liver*, tends to be improperly formed in some way.

We cannot over-emphasize the importance of the liver to the correct functioning and healthy life pattern of every individual. The liver is known by medical science to be responsible for scores of different functions – all of them of great importance to the health of the body. The known functions are only at the material level. There are additional functions at the aetheric and astral levels which the liver also performs, and these are every bit as essential to the health of the individual as those which occur at the material plane.

Thus, the presence of disease, malformation or dysfunction in the liver – regardless of the nature of the problem – always points to a present or previous lopsidedness in the higher self at the *mind* level. We say 'previous' because there are many cases in which a person is born with a defective liver, or has a lingering condition due to some liver illness now in the past, and where that person has fully managed to correct the lopsidedness in his higher part. However, because of the inertia of all matter at the physical plane of being, any formerly diseased part can linger on in a state of illness or sensitivity until the mind and the visualization ability, working together, have corrected the structural problem at the physical level.

Nonetheless, we should emphasize that any *acute* liver condition — including the gall bladder (part of the liver complex) — should normally be taken as a pointer to a concurrent imbalance or lopsidedness in the mental portion of the higher self, probably reflected in the thought patterns or attitudes of the lower personality as well.

The Circulatory System

The *Heart* is the primary organ of this system, which includes the arterial and venous blood passages, the aorta and the spleen. The heart is the organ which is the most closely associated with the heart *chakra*, that location on the aetheric body from which the pure love vibration can be sent forth. Any inability of the heart chakra to function as a fully open center through which the highest love qualities can manifest will lead ultimately to dysfunction, illness or structural incapacitation of this organ.

This applies equally well to congenital failings and damage. The heart organ is literally formed during the foetal stage by tapping the energies of the soul that is intended to occupy the body after birth. Specifically, it the *love* side of the soul that is tapped in this process, and whenever there is a lopsidedness or failing in the love energies at the higher level, this automatically gives rise to a symbolically appropriate problem at the physical level in the heart organ itself. The flaws in the heart can be of many kinds, and it is not appropriate in this text to deal with all of them. However, we can mention a few of the more common heart difficulties.

When the problem manifests as an irregularity in the *rhythm* of the heart, this is signifying an *inconsistency* in the love nature. In other words, one who is not able to maintain his love feeling at a constant level, or who finds that his ability to love comes and goes, will typically develop some form of rhythm problem. This may relate to the rapidity of the heart beat, the sequence in which the valves open, or the strength of

31

the beat itself – any of which may be subject to fluc-
tuation or irregularity.

When the heart problem is in the form of heart *attack*,
usually due to a failure of the blood supply to the
heart muscle, then the symbolic indicator is that the
person has not learned to supply the love side of his
'triangle' with sufficient *energy* (blood = energy). In
other words, the individual is not directing himself as
much as he should to the matter of expressing and
manifesting love in his relations with others. It is
essentially this lesson for which he came to the earth.
Now, there are cases in which a person who has had
heart attacks strikes others as a very loving individual.
However, this would have been acquired in *this life*,
precisely because of the 'reminder' which his weak
heart was meant to provide constantly.

This brings us to an important point. It is not always
correct to assume that the flaws we have pointed to in
this section – the ones being signalled by the various
illness and dysfunctions of the organs – *are still in
need of attention and learning*. In a minority of cases
the presence of the difficulty has had its hoped-for
effect, namely to inspire the victim to put more effort
into learning the relative lesson, to induce him to make
the fundamental changes which are necessary to re-
acquire the balance that had been lost. Therefore, it
is possible to find, for example, very loving individuals
who are nonetheless plagued by heart problems, angina,
or whatever.

Turning now to a third form of heart-related illness,
we wish to discuss the meaning of *circulatory* problems
which involve the *condition of the blood*. The blood is
subject to several irregularities:

High blood pressure is a disease which attacks those
whose love-nature is unevolved. The love capacity is
certainly present, but the individual tends to reserve
that love for only a few others, and does not allow himself to feel love, affection or compassion for a broad
spectrum of his acquaintances. And he is certainly
far away from the realization that his love should be
given out to all of mankind, and indeed all of creation.
The absence of the ability to allow the love nature to
run freely in effect 'dams up' the flow of love. It is
known that when a river is dammed up, the water
level rises higher and higher, the pressure on the dam
increases more and more, until finally something must
break to relieve the pressure. It is precisely this ana-

logy which is being played out for the victim of high blood pressure. Of course, many people pre-dispose themselves to this disease of the blood through improper diet, but the analogy holds true nonetheless. The simplest way to combat hypertension (high blood pressure) is to switch over gradually to a high vegetable, low protein diet, preferably to a vegetarian regime, *and to practice loving all souls that one contacts.* It is essential for the habit of loving everyone to be cultivated, for merely changing the diet alone will not fully achieve the desired cure.

Anaemia is a disease of the blood in which, for any number of apparently physical reasons, the red cell count in the blood is low. The physical causes which have been blamed for this condition are many, but the ultimate spiritual reason for anaemia is the inability and unwillingness to use one's talents and the gifts from God in the service of Love, i.e. the service of one's fellow souls. The red cells of the blood convey energy to the other parts of the body, by carrying oxygen to the cells. The oxygen, which is breathed in through the lungs, represents *energy* pure and simple. The failure of the blood to convey this energy properly is meant to signify that the energy aspect and the love aspect of the individual are not working together correctly. Even some individuals who on the surface are aware of spiritual things may be subject to anaemia. In such a case, the victim must ask himself whether he really is putting this awareness of the higher realities into the service of the race, whether he really is carrying out the task that was assigned for this life and for which he was given the special abilities and gifts. If the answer is no, then that is the explanation – the hidden one – for the presence of the anaemic condition.

Finally there is the blood condition which leads to a hardening of the arteries. While this often strikes older individuals rather than younger, there is nonetheless a perfectly understandable spiritual reason for the condition – which applies equally well regardless of the age of the victim. The hardening of the arteries denotes a *hardening of the emotional side of the individual.* The closing down of a previous openness, the adopting of a 'hardened' feeling toward someone else, these rigidifications of the emotional nature will always predispose a person to hardening of the arteries. The reason why more older people suffer from this disease is now evident: most younger people are able to retain a certain 'suppleness' of emotional response which effectively protects them from this illness. The willingness to be flexible in the affections and emotions ensures that the blood passages themselves will remain supple.

Now, it is also true that the diet followed by most people in the affluent countries pre-disposes them to hardening of the arteries, by robbing the body of those chemical factors which are necessary to allow the arterial walls to remain flexible. Again, the best dietary 'cure' for this condition is to gradually switch to a vegetarian diet which is low in protein generally, although this *must* be accompanied by a 'loosening up' of the emotional rigidness that has been adopted. We must point out, however, that most older people who are subject to this disease are so 'hardened' in their ways, and are such creatures of habit, that attempts to get them to adopt radical changes in diet and in their emotional natures are likely to meet with strong resistance and a certain amount of scoffing and ridicule. We do not say that regeneration is impossible. We are merely trying to warn seekers that the negative habits built up over a long lifetime usually are not broken down in a matter of weeks or months. There must be a strong willingness on the part of the victim to alter his life-pattern radically, and this kind of resolve and commitment in sufferers of arterial hardening is *very* rare.

The Spleen

This organ is less commonly affected than other parts of the circulatory system. Indeed, the spleen is also a part of the lymph system (to be dealth with subsequently) and therefore not all spleen problems will relate directly to the love nature. It is advisable for the seeker to explore the matter carefully before trying to offer the sufferer a spiritual explanation for the problem with his spleen.

Essentially, the spleen is a storehouse for blood. The spleen will discharge into the bloodstream to make up at least a part of that which has been lost. Now, a disease of the spleen will usually though not always refer to a lack of capacity for love at the soul level. This must be considered carefully, however. The matter is often too obscure to allow one to use this knowledge in a directly helpful way for the victim. Simply explore the question carefully and then offer whatever interpretation seems to suggest itself, based on a general knowledge of the body's symbolism.

The Lungs

The lungs are the organs which are responsible for allowing oxygen to enter to the bloodstream. The lungs, however, take in not only oxygen, but *prana* as well. The intake of prana is, in fact, their primary function from an esoteric point of view, for it is this prana which is the true source of most of the body's energy. The substance we are calling prana is not at the physical level, but at the aetheric. It passes directly into the aetheric body with each breath, and from this location can be distributed to the various centers of that body, thence to the corresponding physical organs and body parts.

Whether by reason of the intake of oxygen, or of prana, the esoteric symbology of the lungs is the same: *energy*. Any misuse of energy will tend to predispose the lungs to illness. Here we deal primarily with the *karmic consequences of past life actions*. For example, when a person misused the energy he was given in a previous life, for example by bullying others through his superior strength, then in this life he may be born with defective lungs, or with lungs that are predisposed to developing certain illnesses like tuberculosis, bronchitis, pneumonia, pleurisy and the like. Those who are born with asthmatic conditions are setting aside karma for having brutalized others in a prior life experience on the earth plane. Additionally, it is hoped that, by experiencing the shortness of breath which the asthmatic condition gives rise to, the individual will 'remember' at the subconscious level that he/she once misused energy and will resolve never to do so again. *Allergic* sensitivities of the breathing apparatus often include a factor relating to the misuse of energy, but in some cases the allergy arises from a traumatic experience in the present or a previous life. For example, most cat allergies arise because the sufferer was once mauled or killed by some member of the cat family.

This is an appropriate place to tie in the idea of *shortness of stature* generally. The basic rule relating to the overall size of the physical body is that the size is based on the amount of 'soul-stuff' which is manifesting through it. There are some exceptions, but generally speaking, the more there is to the soul, the larger the body which it must inhabit. Human beings have gradually acquired more and more soul-essence through their various adventures on the earth plane and in other realms – sometimes as a result of a direct gift from a higher plane of being – and this is the reason why the bodies which humanity has used have gradually grown in stature.

The exception arises when a person has misused energy – specifically the body size – in a previous life. When this happens, it is sometimes considered that one way to teach the individual not to make that mistake again is to require him to live a life in a physical body which is 'too small' for the amount of soul-essence trying to manifest through it. During such a life, the person will be haunted by a continual sense of frustration and inadequacy, wishing that he or she were bigger, or stronger, or more 'alive', in some sense. It is difficult to put words to this feeling of frustration, but those who suffer it will recognize immediately what we are referring to.

The Lymph System

Essentially, the lymph system is that which clears out toxins, wastes and poisonous material from the spaces between cells. The lymph empties into the blood stream and thus the toxins collected by the lymph ducts ultimately must be filtered from the blood by the kidneys. When a person fasts, the lymph system collects far more waste material from intercellular regions than is normally the case, and this is the reason why headaches and kidney soreness are common among those fasting for the first time.

Being the system used by the body to rid itself of wastes and toxins, any malfunction of the lymph system may be pointing to an unwillingness on the part of the individual to rid himself of 'wastes' in another sense – the build-up of harmful habits, traits or negativity which are common in those not motivated to cleanse or purify themselves. The refusal comes about usually due to a certain laziness or lack of concern on the part of the negative individual: he sees no reason why he should exert himself to become better, or to stop deleterious habits, or to halt negative patterns of action or thought. The laziness of such an attitude is perfectly reflected in the fact that the lymph system is indeed the most 'sluggish' and slow of all the bodily systems. It has no pump like the heart to move the lymph along; it does not even represent a complete or 'closed' circulatory system. It is simply a series of one-way ducts which ultimately dump their charge of toxin-laden lymph into the blood stream at various points. Instead of having its own lymph-moving apparatus, the lymph sys-

tem relies on other body organs to do its work: the
muscles, the heart and the lungs. Hence, since the
lymph system is a 'tired' system in a sense, any tendency to feel 'tired of it all', or to be tired of some
particular person, fact or circumstance in one's life,
can easily bring about a disease which attacks the lymph
system. The illness known as mononucleosis is one of
the main diseases of the lymph system, and it strikes
only those who have become 'tired' of some person,
facet or thing in their lives, or who have in some manner adopted an attitude of laziness or lack of concern
in some area that needs work or effort. We have given
an example of this particular illness in our book,
Threshold.

The Nervous System

In the body, certain of the general systems correspond to the ancient elements of earth, air, fire and
water, and the latter in turn correspond to the 'humours'
of man, namely the physical, mental, emotional and feeling natures. Thus, the physical level of experience is
represented by the digestive tract and the skeleton.
The mental level is denoted by the respiratory system
(also related to energy, as aforesaid) and the nervous
system. The emotional experience is centered in the
circulatory (blood) system, and the feeling nature is
tied to the lymph network. (The muscular system is a
hybrid in terms of its symbology, relating both to the
physical side and to the emotional.)

The foregoing is by way of pointing out that the
nevous system is basically that which corresponds to
the mental side of man. Any illness or disease which
attacks the nervous system will have some symbolic
meaning in terms of the mental side. Many illnesses of
the nervous system are caused by misuse of mental gifts,
or the development of negative thinking habits. Others
are the result of the misuse of the mind in prior lives.
It is too complicated a matter to detail the usual connec-
tions between specific nervous-related afflictions and
particular mental abuses which give rise to them, but
the interested seeker can determine the general correspondences for himself simply by meditating on the question after carefully determining the *effects* of the various
illnesses, always remembering that most illnesses are
karmic, and are intended to cause the victim to suffer
the same experiences which he had once caused to
another.

37

Chapter 5
The Skeleton

We have already dealt with the bones in the leg.
Those in the foot have various specific meanings which
do not need to be given in this text, since the spiritual
significance is small. They refer mainly to physical
conditions in the body itself, so that a break or deficiency in one of the bones of the foot would point to a
weakness in the corresponding part of the body as a
whole. The seeker can readily determine these connec-
tions for himself, by learning the bones and then by
observing closely those who have problems associated
with those bones.

The bones of the trunk consist primarily of the pelvic
bone, the spine and the ribs. The pelvic bone is a
major pathway along which flow the energies from the
root chakra (that at the base of the spine). As such,
the pelvic bone directly represents the creative and
pro-creative aspects of the self. When there is any
chronic problem associated with this bone, as happens
in many older persons, it is certain that the root chakra
energies are not flowing properly. This may be due to
a damming up of these energies through the operation
of certain insidious thought-patterns often connected
with prudishness, though in many cases where older
persons develop weakness of the pelvic bone, the difficulty arises because of improper diet over many de-
cades, combined with negative emotional states that
have become habitual. Such conditions cause terrible
depredations throughout the physical body, and there-

fore it is no wonder that the power available in the various chakras is diminished.

The spine relates to a large number of basic soul
qualities. We will attempt to detail a number of these
correspondences, but wish to point out first in a general
way that, just as the soul has three facets (the physical,
the emotional and the mental), so the vertebrae of the
spine are divided into 1) a lower group relating to the
'physical' side of the soul, 2) a middle group denoting
the 'emotional' traits of the soul, and 3) an upper group
denoting the 'mental' side of the soul. At the soul level
or the higher self these meanings are not exactly the
same as the corresponding facets of the lower self or
personality, but their nature does strongly influence
the characteristics which manifest through the lower
self.

The 'physical' vertebrae include the coccyx (a group
of three to five vestigeal vertebrae fused together at
the base of the spine), the sacrum (the five vertebrae
above the coccyx — also fused together), and the next
seven vertebrae in order counting upwardly. The latter
involve the five lumbar vertebrae and the bottom two
thoracic vertebrae. The fused vertebrae in the coccyx
and the sacrum have a direct relationship with the traits
of the physical body which are 'fixed' and cannot be
significantly changed during an incarnation. Hence the
'fused' nature of these vertebrae. The lowest ones of
the fused vertebrae correspond to the skeleton of the
body. The bones are the densest, hardest substances
in the body, and thus are the most akin to the earth
level of manifestation. Their counterpart facets at the
higher self level are those which influence strongly the
nature of the skeleton as a whole, in terms of its relative strength and its resistance to disease and malfunction. Here, then, is a microcosm of the skeleton of the
body.

The upper fused bones relate to the circulatory system as a whole, for this too is a system whose basic
nature tends to remain fixed and unchanging throughout life. This is not to say that the resistance of the
veins or arteries to ailments cannot be improved. What
we are referring to is the relative ease or difficulty
with which this system can be affected by dietary
change and mental procedures.

The next three vertebrae (the lower three lumbar v.)
pertain to the respiratory system, including the lungs
and breathing passages. Above these, the next three

relate to the musculature of the body, while the last
(the second thoracic from the bottom, or T-11) relates
to the digestive system.

It will be appreciated that damage (whether permanent or passing) to any of these vertebrae, or any
chronic deficiency, dysfunction or pain originating
there, will designate a portion or system of the body
which is below par, diseased or chronically deficient
in some way.

Moving now to the 'emotional' vertebrae, these include
the rest of the thoracic vertebrae (T-1 to T-10) and the
lowermost cervical vertebra (C-7). These eleven vertebrae bear a direct relation with the emotional responses
and traits of the manifested personality, because they
pertain to those characteristics of the higher self which
are responsible for the traits at the lower level.

Beginning with the lower four of this group (T-7 to
T-10), these correspond to the ability to love, pure
and simple. Any person who has a problem in these
vertebrae must ask himself whether he has the ability
to allow the pure love emotion – untainted by any
thought of sexual passion, self-pleasure or physical
indulgence – to flow through his heart chakra. It is
essential for the reader to grasp this thought, for in
the world today too many think they love when in reality their experience is primarily based in the desire
nature and the proclivities of the physical body. Hence,
many call 'love' what is really only physical infatuation.
Love does not desire, it merely loves. Love seeks not
to be always with the loved one, only that the loved
one should be happy. Love requires no returned emotion of loyalty or affection, it merely sends out its loving rays, knowing that all love returns finally to the
source of everything, which is God. How many can say
that their love nature is capable of such selfless affection? Very few. And yet that is the goal for man, in
terms of developing and manifesting the love of God, or
Christ-Love. Any who find it impossible to generate
such a feeling of unconditional love within themselves,
may find that the corresponding bones of the spine are
in some manner deficient, subject to disease, out of
alignment, or simply the source of backache.

The next three of the 'emotional' vertebrae (T-4 to
T-6) pertain not to love per se, but rather to the
ability to feel joy and elation while in physical incarnation. The usual manifestation of this trait is in the
sense of humor and the ability to laugh, these being

very high characteristics which belong more properly on the angelic planes. Indeed, the gift of laughter was made to man as a deliberate act some hundreds of thousands of years ago, for prior to that gift man was unable to laugh and could never see the point of a joke. He was much more akin to the animals in terms of his emotions, and like them was unable to laugh. Hence, troubles relating to the vertebrae in question point to one whose sense of humor may be either lacking or rudimentary. We should point out here that there are many degrees of such troubles. Sometimes a minor problem in these vertebrae is used by one's guides merely to remind the person subconsciously that he should allow more fun, lightness and laughter into his life. Those who tend to be overly serious, even though they may have a good sense of humor, often find that these particular vertebrae give them trouble. In such cases, the individual must assess for himself whether the indicator is merely a reminder to laugh more, or whether some more serious imbalance is being pointed out: The same caution applies to the interpretation of all of the vertebrae correspondences.

The next three vertebrae in order, counting upwardly, are those identified as T-1 to T-3 (the upper three thoracic v.). These bones pertain to another of the 'highest' emotional traits in man, namely his ability to rise above the limitations of physical existence on the wings of *hope*. This emotion is akin to faith in many ways, and thus we may say that the ability to keep faith and hope alive in the midst of adversity is represented by the vertebrae in question. Those who have adopted a despairing attitude toward life, or who have given up hope regarding their lot, are those most likely to experience pain or difficulty in association with these three vertebrae.

The final one of the 'emotional' vertebrae is C-7, namely the lowest cervical vertebra. This bone relates to another evolved 'emotion', namely that of *praise*. This is a difficult concept to describe in any other terms. The English word praise is one of unclear meaning for most people, who have never allowed themselves to be flooded by the currents of praise which, for example, the Angels constantly feel toward the Highest Creator. In many religious books the notion of praise is discussed, but few now understand its meaning. We will attempt to describe this feeling, in the hopes that some will be encouraged to make it a part of their daily

42

experience, and thus reap the great rewards that come from allowing these special currents to flow through one's being.

"Praise the Lord!" is an expression that many are familiar with. It tends to be regarded as the watchword of certain religious fundamentalists who allow themselves to be overcome with devotional frenzy, thus losing control of themselves to the point where this and other spontaneous phrases are shouted.

And yet a beautiful jewel lies within this thought, i.e. that one should praise the Lord. The value of the notion stems from the fact that in allowing this emotion to flood one's higher bodies, a closeness to the Creator is established that cannot be erected in any other way.

We will be more specific. The approach to God can take place along different vibrations. We have pointed out elsewhere that, at the *mental* level, one can grasp the true nature of the Godhead only to a limited degree, depending upon one's own development and advancement. By contrast, on the emotional vibration, a complete integration and interchange can take place between God and any of His creatures. The emotional side of reality, however, has many sub-realms. The pure *love* emotion directed at the Godhead will always and immediately call forth a returned flood of love to the one sending it out. Any who care to try sending pure love aloft to the Creator will be flooded in return with His own love, and usually some physical signal of this return will be felt: a tingling in the spine, or a sensation in the chakras of the heart or head, or a somewhat euphoric feeling.

By comparison, the directing of *praise* toward the Godhead (another facet of the emotional side) accomplishes something different. It brings the sender into contact with that part of the Creator which is responsible for the bounty and beauty which surround man. By practicing praise, the human soul calls to itself an abundance of all that is good, as the Creator seeks to 'answer' the call that has gone out.

It must here be understood that *God always seeks to respond to His creatures in kind.* For love, He returns love. For mental communication, He replies in a way that the mind can grasp. For praise, however, the only appropriate response is to shower upon the one praising Him an abundance of that which the soul requires in life. Any who care to make this test will quickly see that it brings results.

Of course, the matter cannot be undertaken with the ulterior motive of acquiring riches or abundance. The feeling of praise for the Godhead must be absolutely genuine, for otherwise it will not reach to that high level.

Now, many persons are not able to say just what the attitude of 'praising God' is like, because they have never before given it much thought. The idea is merely to allow the heart to fill to overflowing with gratitude and homage to the ultimate Creator who is responsible for all that one sees, for the universe itself, and indeed for the creation of one's own soul. It is a mixture of thankfulness, a prayerful attitude, a sense of the sheer glory of the Most High, and a real component of the *usual* notion of praise, i.e. the holding in mind of the wondrous attributes of the Father: His power, His Greatness, His Love, His Mercy, His Everlasting Being, etc. If the seeker but tries to encompass these ideas with his mind and heart, he will find that it is truly possible to 'Praise the Lord'.

We turn now to the mental facets as represented by the upper vertebrae of the spine, those referred to conventionally as the top six cervical vertebrae (C-1 to C-6). The lowest of these is C-6, which refers to the mental ability to rationalize, reason and solve problems in logic. Its position at the bottom of the row of 'mental' vertebrae comes not by chance. Seen in a spiritual perspective, the logical nature of man's mind is the least significant of its capacities. After all, any computer can be taught to think in purely logical terms, and no inner spiritual essence is required for that form of mental activity.

The next vertebra in order is C-5, which denotes the capacity for seizing the whole of a concept at one grasp – this being the gift which is related astrologically to strong aspects between Mercury and Uranus. In its essential nature, this is almost an *intuitive* capability for it actually by-passes the more plodding logical faculty by leaping ahead to the full comprehension of that which is contemplated.

Following this is C-5, which has a direct connection with the talent usually ascribed to instinctive or sub-conscious capacities, namely that of 'knowing' the inner essence or truth of a thing. In actual fact, this 'knowing' stems from a contact with the soul-mind or higher mind, which sees from a far loftier perspective than the physical plane of matter. This contact brings the vertebral association up to the level of the soul or higher self, and the remaining mental vertebrae also have their meanings at this higher level.

C-3, the next cervical vertebra, relates directly to the capacity for *perceiving spiritual truth*, as this exists in the higher self, and as it is echoed down to the lower personality. The perception and acceptance of spiritual truth when this is encountered is one of the most important abilities on the earth plane, for it literally allows the soul to steer its way safely among the shoals of temptation, and avoid the traps which reality holds out for the unwary. All too many people fall readily into these snares, for they lack the discernment and discrimination which alone can safeguard the soul on its pilgrimage through incarnation.

The vertebra next above C-3 is known conventionally as the axis, and is numbered C-2. It is the bone on which the head turns from side to side in a pivoting motion. Due to this function, it will be understandable to those who grasp symbolism that the axis represents the ability to develop a *breadth* of understanding and comprehension. Upon this bone, the head can turn from one side to another, and in an analogous way the bone represents the capacity to rise above narrowness of conception, restrictions of thought and the blind prejudices which so characterize present-day mankind.

Finally comes C-1, which is known as the atlas. This bone supports the entire weight of the skull, and in particular allows the head to nod up and down due to its interface with the occipital condyles. Symbolically, the atlas refers to the spark of divine intellect which lies at the very center of the mind of man, and from which the other capacities and abilities of a mental nature have developed. Hence, the topmost bone of the spinal column denotes that part of man's mental faculty which is from God – the fragment of the Creator's own mind which He has given as a gift to each human being. How appropriate that the bone which allows man to nod his head forward in a prayerful attitude is that which denotes the divine spark of mind within him!

Our survey of the spinal vertebrae is now complete. It will moreover be obvious to the reader that any serious debility affecting a given vertebra will be a pointer directly to the facet or capacity which corresponds, suggesting that the individual give some thought to the area being designated. By so doing, he may be able to perceive areas which require effort

and improvement, and through this understanding
of symbolic meaning some benefit to the soul may
accrue.

We wish now to offer a relatively complete course in
palmistry, however with the proviso that we will not
dwell overly long on areas which are already generally
understood and available in the standard texts. It is
through the study of the human hand that man can
most rapidly come to an understanding of himself,
his purpose, the lessons which he must learn in incarnation, and the weaknesses that stand as dangers and
traps to lure him away from the true path.

Chapter 6
The Background

We have explained at the beginning of this book that
the triple threads of mental, emotional and physical
experience intertwine continuously through man's incarnations on the earth plane. In the symbology of the
palm, these three golden lines literally condense onto
the surface of the palm, forming the head line, the heart
line and the life line. Reference may be had to Figure
5. These three lines show directly the nature of the
mental, emotional and physical components of the individual, at least in terms of the tendencies with which he
was born. In some cases a person will learn to rise
above the limitations and difficulties which may be drawn
upon these lines, but such cases are unfortunately few.
There is little understanding among mankind today that
the purpose of life is to correct failings, to modify lop-
sided tendencies, and to learn the great spiritual lessons
that incarnation offers.

But there is much more on the human hand as well.
For example, the subconscious of each individual
stretches down along the edge of the hand under the
little finger; the more prominent past lives are drawn
as shadow lines parallel to the life line within the ball of
the thumb; and achievements in terms of the major life
lessons learned in past incarnations are symbolized by
the whorl patterns at the ends of the fingers.

We propose to deal with all of these areas in detail,
but first we wish to explain the process by which the
lines and other marks of the hand are arranged, and
the purpose behind this magnificent and complex system of meaning.

How the Lines are Created

When the foetus is developing in its mother's womb, and after it is known for certain which soul shall occupy the body after birth, steps are undertaken to place a preliminary sketch of the major hand lines upon the palms, and to mark the fingers in an appropriate way. Much can be seen ahead of time in terms of general characteristics and the probable major events in the life about to be lived. When this information has been assembled, and after the foetal hands have been sufficiently formed (this happens at about five months), angel entities who specialize in the area of palmistry arrange to make the required impressions and patterns on the *aetheric* body of the foetus, knowing that the natural laws will cause such markings to appear also on the physical hands within a short time. First, however, these entities devise a basic pattern for the palmar lines which will accurately represent the character and traits of the personality complex which is about to be projected. The major tendencies can always be worked out relatively accurately by merely inspecting the patterns which have developed in past incarnations of the same soul. Such observations form the basis for the major line directions and forms. However, the smaller 'influence' lines — those which touch the major lines — are usually rather few at this early stage. It is true that some newborns show a plethora of such influence lines (which mainly denote specific events planned for the individual in this incarnation), but in most cases the infant hands are relatively barren of such lines.

As the individual grows and develops a specific personality pattern, his guides can determine more accurately what kinds of events are both necessary and possible for him to undergo, and when these decisions have become firm, the same angel entities are asked to modify or add to the hand patterns in accordance with what is now planned. This they do while the individual sleeps at night. The changes are made in the *astral* hands, and the modifications soon appear on the physical counterparts. The angels must use the aetheric body during gestation, due to the fact that the foetus does not have a well-defined astral body of its own. In essence, it shares and is protected by the mother's astral body. However, after about age two, the angels then can use this more preferred way of influencing the hand markings.

This process of modification continues throughout life, as the individual changes, learns lessons or backslides, makes his various choices, etc. Even the major lines can be seen to change, especially at their ends, over periods of six months to a year. Any who care to keep a record of their handprints over an extended period will soon see that such changes do occur.

Indeed, there is no better way to learn palmistry than to constantly inspect one's own hands – to watch as the smaller markings come and go – and to *think* about what it all might mean. Every scar, every bruise, cut, pinch, wart and spot, has its story to tell, its warning or lesson to convey. Each influence line, the striations which run along the finger phalanges, and the patterns at the end of the fingers – all of these hide a great wealth of meaning for the seeker who has put the necessary effort into learning to read the significance of the human palm.

We will start this course in palmistry by looking at the ends of the fingers – at the ridge patterns which are used by criminologists to keep track of lawbreakers.

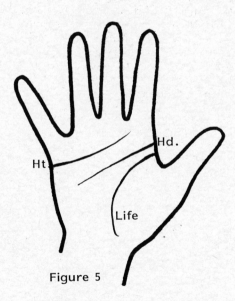

Figure 5

Chapter 7

The Finger-end Patterns

Each of the five fingers has a direct symbolic relation
to one of the five major lesson-learning areas which incarnation offers to human souls. The patterns seen on
the end or nail phalanges of the fingers tell of accomplishments – or the lack of them – in previous life experiences on the earth plane. Let us begin with the little
finger and work across to the thumb.

The Little Finger
This finger is under the general rulership of the
planet Mercury, which in Astrology relates to the mental
traits, business, interchanges of all kinds and communication. In palmistry, while these key ideas have some
relevance, the most important connotation for the
Mercury finger is that of the *sexual lessons*. There is
a subtle derivation of this connotation, based on considering Mercury as essentially a bisexual god or symbol. In astrology, a deeper level of significance recog-
nizes in Mercury the 'androgynous' principle, i.e. the
concept of having the male and female characteristics
together in one being. Hence the rulership of Gemini
by Mercury – Gemini meaning the twins (a male and
female). Now, considering that Gemini/Mercury bring
the two sexual roles together into one package, it might
now be understood that – in terms of palmistry – the
significance of the Mercury rulership has to do with
sorting out the confusions and ambivalences which arise
from the fact that every soul – and every incarnate
personality – combines the two sexes within itself in
terms of traits and general tendencies. Let us be more
specific.

Most of the difficulty which arises in connection with
sex derives from the fact that men try too hard to suppress their female side, while women often inhibit their
natural desire to allow their male traits to manifest.
We are not suggesting that men become effeminate or
that women become mannish. What we are referring to
is that the male 'package' of aggressiveness, sportive-
ness, rational intellect and ambition are present in all
personalities, whether male or female in sexual gender;
and that the female traits of intuitiveness, the nurtur-
ing instinct, demonstrativeness in the affections and
gentleness of manner are likewise present in all souls
incarnate upon the earth plane. Difficulties in the sexual inter-relationships between souls arise primarily
because of a misunderstanding of the essentially androgynous nature of the soul, and because individuals seek
to disguise, suppress or contort traits and characteristics which are quite natural to them.

Naturally, other forms of sexual disharmony can result
from the misuse of sexual energy for purely pleasure
motives, or to dominate another soul, or to bind another
soul against its will.

All of these misuses of sexual energy represent a
failure to understand and learn the sexual lesson which
the earth plane has to offer: namely that the sexual
interchange between two souls that are 'mated' in affection and mental attitude is the supreme form of sharing
between those two individuals, and was meant to be an
oasis of joy and respite to which the souls could turn
as a counterpoint to the demands and stress of a busy
life. The secret of success in sexual terms is to 'give
up the self', and concentrate on bringing happiness to
the partner. All difficulties on the earth stem ultimately
from the prodominance of the selfish attitude, and the
sexual area is no exception. If individuals would
learn to look on the sexual interchange as an opportunity
to *give* something of value to another soul, most of the
so-called sexual hang-ups would disappear. Indeed,
any who care to change their attitudes in the direction
indicated would quickly find that even greater pleasure
is the reward for both partners.

We must finally stress that the sex act must not be
undertaken with a person for whom no genuine affection
is felt. For, unless the heart chakra too is open, the
root chakra (that which furnishes all of the sexual
energy) is unable to operate properly, and only tension
and dissatisfaction can result. Any attempt to prompt

the body alone to stir up the sexual impulse is also
doomed to failure in the sense of real fulfillment. The
body was meant to be the *follower* in the sexual interchange, not the leader. Unless the body's sexual role
is merely that of allowing the soul to express a love
and affection already felt at other levels (mental and
emotional), no enduring relationship can be built and
nothing of lasting value can be achieved.

Turning to the markings at the end of the little finger,
we wish to identify the three basic pattern types which
represent 'stages of learning'. The most advanced stage
is represented by the whorl, of which two types are
shown in Figure 6. The middle stage in learning is denoted by the loop pattern, shown in Figure 7. Finally
a rudimentary stage is indicated by the simple ridge,
as illustrated in Figure 8. There are other gradations
as well, representing stages between the ones already
described, and with a little practice the seeker should
quickly learn to distinguish all the levels and rank
them in order of 'success'.

Now, we must emphasize that the patterns at the finger ends do not tell of accomplishments in the *present*
life. Nor could they, because they are 'set' at the time
of birth and do not change during a given incarnation.
What these patterns designate is the *maximum that had
ever been achieved during previous incarnations* with
respect to the particular lesson being pointed to.

Let us give an example. Suppose a person has a
whorl pattern on the little finger, resembling the patterns in Figure 6. Now, this would indicate that, regardless of the further learning or *unlearning* that
might have taken place in the present life, the maximum attained in any *previous* incarnation — i.e. the
best that was ever accomplished in terms of learning
the right, balanced approach to sexual experience —
was near to the maximum possible. It is important to
realize that such a sign might well be found on the little
finger of someone given to sexual abuse, perversion,
or whatever. A previous success in some other life
does not always guarantee that the same high standard
can be maintained. The matter is even more complex.
Suppose that this individual, despite his previous
high level of learning in this particular lesson, wished
to *test* his ability to see the truth in the present incarnation. As a result, this individual might have con-
sented to be born under certain *filters* or *overlays*
which had the effect of making it particularly difficult

to successfully navigate the stormy seas of sexual desire and obsession. For example, the personality might have been born deliberately under the astrological pattern of Mars in Scorpio or Mars in Capricorn. This influence, regardless of the inborn 'balance' that might have been passed down from the soul or higher self, could well 'unbalance' the personality traits to the extent that a sexual overemphasis, obsession or perversion might arise. However, the soul could well have undertaken this particularly difficult 'program' deliberately... possibly to *test* its ability. Perhaps the soul was not completely satisfied that the learning was fully balanced. Or perhaps the soul wished to offset further karma by dragging itself through the imbalance in the sexual area and suffering the inevitable pain and sorrow which come to those who abuse themselves or others in the sexual sense.

And perhaps, when this incarnation is through, that soul will have learned even better than previously that one should not stress the self in the sexual area, that the sexual embrace was meant to allow souls to *give* to each other, not to *take* from each other, and that if one allows the body's natural sexual function to *follow* the cue given it by an open, loving heart, then no sorrow or sadness can result.

Before turning to the other four fingers, we will discuss the question of the appearance of different patterns on the same finger of two hands. Suppose an individual has a whorl pattern on the right hand little finger, and a loop on the left. Now, in connection with these patterns the rule to follow is this: The right hand denotes a more recent life pattern, and the left denotes one farther back. This is the case regardless of the hand with which the person writes. Thus in our example, the whorl on the right hand denotes a recent success, and suggests that the summit of the learning for this lesson occurred relatively recently. Possibly, the soul had a recent life in which that lesson was the main point of concentration, and hence rapid progress was made. If the left hand had only a ridge pattern (Fig. 8) while the right had a whorl (a rare occurrence), the meaning would be that the learning was quite abrupt and quite recent. In other words, prior to the 'success' life in terms of the sexual lesson, the individual was quite elementary and 'unawakened' in his approach to the whole area of sex. But because of that particular recent life, much was assimilated in a very brief time (measured against the whole of the reincarnational sequence of lives).

Now, suppose the person had the reversed arrangement. In such case, the advanced marking on the left hand denotes success at a more distant time in the past, while the less advanced mark on the right tells that the previous learning was to some extent lost or 'unlearned' in a more recent experience on the earth plane. Neither of these indications allows the hand reader to conclude the stage at which the individual has attained in the *present* life. These patterns merely tell the state of affairs at the *beginning* of this life. Naturally, if there are any areas of major learning yet to be mastered, it is expected that the soul will make the effort and accomplish what is required. The fact that, at mankind's present primitive stage, most individuals fail to learn even half of the lessons which are 'set' for each incarnation, is no justification for concluding that the individual whose hands are being read has likewise simply remained at the previous level of accomplishment. While this will often be the case, it is not to be automatically assumed. And when an individual is found whose level of learning a lesson *does* correspond with a finger pattern which is less than the maximum that can be indicated, then the 'reader' should take the opportunity to explain the lesson still in need of work, in the hopes that by understanding the lesson at the conscious level, the individual will be encouraged to put more effort into the learning than he has thus far done. In this way can the study of palmistry allow one soul to be a spiritual help to another.

Many situations will be found in which the right interpretation is somewhat obscure. In such cases, the seeker is expected silently to consult his own intuition and ask his guides for help with the interpretation. Then, whatever is given should be stated. If it is wrong or does not 'make sense' to the person whose hand is being read, then do not worry about it. His conscious mind will not harbour that to which it cannot relate and no damage will be done. But in most cases, something of value can be derived in this way, and even if the conscious mind rejects what is said, the kernel of truth will sink into the subconscious, and some positive benefit will result.

We now turn to the other four fingers, on the understanding that the basic approach is always the same for all fingers; only the lessons are different.

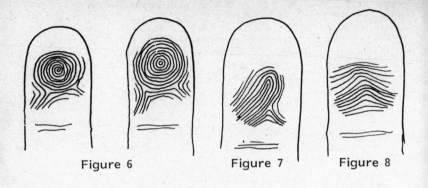

Figure 6   Figure 7   Figure 8

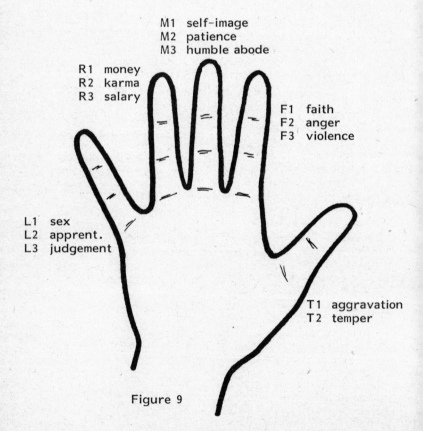

M1   self-image
M2   patience
M3   humble abode

R1   money
R2   karma
R3   salary

F1   faith
F2   anger
F3   violence

L1   sex
L2   apprent.
L3   judgement

T1   aggravation
T2   temper

Figure 9

The Ring Finger

The markings on the end phalange of this finger relate to the lesson of *money*, pure and simple. The great importance of this lesson in the present day will be self-evident. Never before in man's history has there been such temptation to turn the attention solely upon the goods of the world and the money required to obtain them. Nor is it difficult to accumulate a reasonable store of money if sufficient effort is expended. Even for those disinclined to work, it is possible to obtain money from other sources: unemployment insurance, old age benefits, and loan and finance companies. The ready availability of money in present day civilization is meant to make more acute and revealing the *test of money*, i.e. the ability of each individual to avoid the pitfalls of attitude and action which represent a failure in this important test.

The best approach to money is simple to regard it as a necessary factor in the present-day life, one that must be dealt with, something that must be handled due to the fact that, through money, one acquires the ability to purchase the necessities of life. An individual must have access to money in order to care for his loved ones and to provide the basics for himself and those who are dependent upon him. However, any exaggerated emphasis on the importance of money for its own sake, any tendency to see one's own worth or value in terms of the money one has accumulated, any habit of cheating others of their money, of setting exhorbitant prices in order to enrich the self, of using money to control or enslave others – all of these represent a failure in relation to the money lesson.

As with the little finger, the whorl pattern signifies a high level of success in some prior life, the loop represents a middle level of learning, and the simple hump or ridge denotes a primitive level with much yet to be learned. Again, do not forget that these patterns at the finger ends do not tell of the *present* life (in which much may have been learned already) but only point to levels attained in the lives prior to the present. Also, the approach to interpreting a divergence between left and right hand patterns remains as previously explained.

The Middle Finger

The middle finger relates to the lesson of the self-image. The development of a positive self-picture, a secure and confident image of oneself, is of such

over-riding importance to success in terms of earth
incarnation, that we could not possibly over-emphasize
it. In particular, its importance to those on the *Path*
is especially great, for without a happy self-image –
a basic contentment with oneself – very few of the
tests which are applied to seekers could be successfully navigated. We do not propose to deal with the
major tests for seekers, as we have already explained
these in depth in our earlier book, *Dark Robes, Dark
Brothers*.

He who is happy to be with and by himself has a
rich gift – one that he has given himself. Back in
the dawn of the human race, individuals did not real-
lize that they were capable of an independent existence apart from the tribal or racial group. Each person saw himself first and foremost as an integer within
a larger whole, and indeed the concept of the self
as it is now understood was completely unknown. No-
body could have conceived of placing himself before
the group in importance; none could have grasped
the current emphasis on one's own rights, happiness
and will power.

But as the aeons passed, the experiences of the race
gradually taught to all human souls the distinction between each one and the group, between each person
and each other. We have dealt with this process of
differentiation and self-realization in our earlier books,
and we have not the space here to go into the matter
again. Suffice it to say that the end result of the
myriad of experiences through which the human race
put itself was the development of a strong sense of
the self and of the distinctions between souls. However, even though the *concept* of the self was learned
by all, not all were equally happy with the picture or
image which they were able to form of themselves.
There remain today many souls upon the earth who
are not at all content to be by themselves, who think
little of themselves, who see themselves as unworthy,
unclean, unlovable, etc.

In many cases these poor self-images are the fault
of the parents, who have told the individual repeatedly (during his childhood years) that he was "no
good", or unlovable, or whatever. Few parents realize the horrendous damage which they inflict upon
their offspring with these cutting words. The child
literally forms his views of himself on the basis of
what the parents tell him. If he is told repeatedly

that he is unworthy or "bad" or ugly, then his self-picture becomes scarred. These hurtful words go into the subconscious of the child, and unless he learns when he is an adult to *undo* the subconscious damage – by re-programming the bad tapes that were placed there by his parents – it is likely that he will spend an entire incarnation thinking negatively about himself. This will often lead to drinking or drug problems, cruelty towards others in order to temporarily 'beef up' the self-image, and other pitiful modes of behavior.

Hence, there are two possible sources of a poor self-image: damage inflicted by the parents, and an actual feeling of unworthiness at the higher self or soul level. In regard to the latter, such a poor self-image often arises due to feelings of guilt about actions carried out in a previous experience. In other cases, the afflicted self-picture comes about due to the fact that a recent life was cut short at an early age, through a mistake or a misjudgement on the part of the individual. There are many causes of a residual feeling of unworthiness at the level of the higher self, and we do not have space to list them all.

Of more advantage would be an attempt to explain how a poor self-image can be corrected, because the procedure is relatively simple. The way to improve the self-image is to concentrate on one's *good* points, one's *abilities*, one's *successes*. Too many people are in the habit of dwelling on their failures, their mistakes and their disadvantages. The latter habit merely *reinforces* their already poor self-image, and is certainly not calculated to bring about any alleviation of their difficulty. Instead, by concentrating on one's good attributes, one gradually instills into the subconscious mind a different 'tape' than the one which was either built by the parental disapproval or brought in from the higher self at birth.

Specifically, we recommend that anyone suffering from a poor self-image firstly draw up a list of all his good qualities, his successes, and his talents. Even if the list has to be 'padded' a bit, that is all right. There should be at least twenty entries in the list. Then each night before falling asleep and each morning before getting out of bed, consult the list and carefully contemplate each entry. Feel *good* about each of the points in turn. Take at least half a minute for each entry, so that the total time spent in this endeavor is at least ten minutes. We can guarantee

that the expenditure of time will be well rewarded.
After about two weeks, the experimenter will find that
his mind tends to turn to the list entries by itself –
during the day. Suddenly, the mind will fasten upon
one of the good points which are listed, and the idea
will come unbidden into one's consciousness. This is
the signal that the subconscious has memorized the list,
and is in the process of replacing the old negative
images with the new, more positive ones. When this
stage is reached, one should deliberately begin to
spend time by oneself, attempting to maintain a feeling
of contentment and happiness during the time of isolation. These periods of isolation do not have to be of
extended duration. We recommend that they begin at
about thirty minutes only. Each individual may have
his own preference for the way in which these periods
of isolation are to be spent. The best setting for
most people will be one surrounded by the beauty of
nature. There is no more perfect way to come to a
sense of the 'rightness' of the world than to take a
stroll through the woods or along a lakeshore – *by
oneself*. While this activity is being carried out,
strive to maintain an inner feeling of contentment
and peace. The preparation which has preceded this
new phase – i.e. the work on the list of good points
– should now make it relatively simple to be alone
and be happy in that state.

We now wish to suggest a final phase in the program
of improving one's self-image. This involves increasing one's communication with a higher realm of being.
For many this can be done by setting aside certain
regular periods of prayer. For others, meditation is
the way to proceed. For still others, the contact with
the higher realms can come about simply by increasing
one's *awareness* of the myraid other realms and other
kingdoms which surround man on the earth. Our book,
Other Kingdoms, may be found to be helpful for those
wishing to follow the latter path.

Having now dealt with the *lesson* which the middle
finger relates to, we wish to point out that the most
common scenario for *testing* one's ability to be happy
with oneself pertains to the breaking up or threatening of one's personal relationship – whether marriage
or whatever. It is the case that many individuals who
have a poor self-image turn to a personal relationship
as a means of compensating them for their feeling of
inadequacy or unworthiness. Unfortunately, many

souls pair up together who *both* suffer from the same failing in terms of self-image. As such, they tend to lean upon each other, to count on each other to give them the feeling of completeness which they lack. Such relationships are very precarious, because of that dependency. While it was *intended* that humans should pair up in a marriage-like relationship for the purpose of procreation, mutual help and the flowering of affection, the pair-bond is misused if it is counted upon to complete a self-image that is lacking in some way. This is why, whenever any individual launches himself on the *Path*, as it is called, one of the first 'tests' likely to come along is that of his self-image — specifically by having his then current personal relationship or pair-bond get into trouble. It is rare that two persons who had established a pair-bond before either sets his feet upon the Path to spiritual achievement would *both* decide to take this step at the same time. Often, as we have explained in *Dark Robes, Dark Brothers*, the partner who has not chosen the Path will give the other an ultimatum: "It's me or all this spiritual stuff", is the common cry. Then the choice must be made.

A particularly important secret for developing a strong positive self-image is that of *allowing both sides of one's sexuality to manifest*. It is generally understood that each individual, regardless of the sexual identity of the body, has *both* the male and female sides to his nature. However, many men tend to overly suppress any of their responses which smack of the 'female', while many women deny their masculine urges. For example, the 'great athlete' syndrome among men, the 'jock mentality', the hunter/fisherman attitude — these are often found together with a deliberate suppression of any feelings of affection or tenderness toward others. Often too, the sexual side of the man's nature expresses itself mainly in terms of dominance, and little true caring or consideration is manifested. In the case of many women, there is a tendency to suppress their natural desires to compete athletically, to be adventurous, or to seek success in terms of the worldly ambitions. This they do in order not to appear unattractive to men who might feel threatened by such 'unfeminine' behavior. But, aside from the distinctive physical roles in the sexual embrace itself, there is literally nothing which is 'unfeminine' or 'unmasculine'. Why should any soul deny itself the right to enjoy the thrill of athletic competition, or the feeling of having contributed something of value to the world? Likewise, why should any individual refuse to acknowledge his feelings of tenderness and caring toward another, or deny that he has intuitive feelings and an access to knowledge that does not come directly from the reasoning process?

In the age to come, it is expected that men and women will both allow all of their internal characteristics to flower, for that flowering will be the crown of the Aquarian Ideal, as each soul positively encourages all others to spread their wings, to soar into levels of experience and achievement never before tasted, and to find in that expansion of the spirit the key to self-understanding that has been missing for all the centuries.

The Forefinger

The lesson related to the forefinger is that of *Faith*. The end phalange in particular designates the matter of faith in a creative entity or level beyond man, whether this be called God, or Creative Intelligence, or whatever. The important thing is to have some concept of a reality which rises beyond the mundane, physical plane in grandeur, a creative source which is above man in the scheme of things. Those who cannot allow themselves to believe in a God-concept of some kind are showing that their grasp of the true structure of reality is limited. The knowledge regarding higher levels rises always from within the Heart-knowledge which each soul has as a birthright. Any who deny this concept have allowed the merely rational mind to over-rule what the heart knows for a certainty. And by allowing this censorship to operate within them, such souls are cutting off the greatest source of sanity for the lower mind: its support upon the sure pedestal of eternity. The mind alone can never plumb the depths of the mysteries of creation. There are not enough 'givens' for this to take place. Instead, the mind's proper function is to understand, elaborate and categorize the scheme and structure of the totality of creation, after the individual has first become persuaded of its existence by the operation of the heart-wisdom. For there are things which can only be sensed by the Love-wisdom which rises from the heart center, things which would normally be rejected by the cold, rational intellect. Indeed, the scientific attitude which characterizes the twentieth century mode of thought is that which rejects all truths which arise from within the heart center. It is for this reason that the scientific development of of the current century has run out of forward motion. It has not allowed those intuitive *aperçus* of truth from the heart side of man to influence to a sufficient degree the direction of its development.

Returning to the forefinger, then, we will say simply that man's faith in God or a higher principle of creativity is that which is designated by the pattern on the end phalange. As with the other fingers, the maximum degree of success ever attained with this lesson in prior lives is read by observing the ridge patterns in accordance with the scheme shown in Figures 6, 7 and 8.

The Thumb

Finally, the thumb is that which designates man's ability to avoid irritation with the factors in life which tend to exasperate or annoy him. These factors include people, situations, events, etc. The Christ counselled others to 'turn the other cheek', and it is precisely this ability which constitutes success in learning the lesson designated by the end phalange of the thumb. In many ways it is the most difficult of the life lessons represented by the fingers. The thumb itself is the strongest and the most articulate of the digits on the hand, and likewise it represents a lesson which, for many people, requires the greatest degree of effort. How many readers of this book can honestly say that they are never aggravated, annoyed or resentful against others or against the irritations of life? How many have truly learned to 'offer up' these aggravations, to sweep their minds and hearts clean of resentment, or to 'turn the other cheek', as the Master advised. In truth, there are far too few upon the earth today who even understand that such an attitude is desirable. Many seem to have the idea that it is *right* to resent those who have done them some injustice, and that it is proper to return dislike for dislike and enmity for enmity. The petty aggravations of life are pounced upon as excuses for allowing all the nastiness and negativity harbored in the soul to manifest. Is there any wonder that the world is about to set itself alight in the greatest outpouring of wrath and hatred ever seen?

The secret of success in this, the hardest of the lessons for most people, is to understand that resentment and aggravation have only negative effects on the physical and higher bodies, and to resolve once and for all to make a sincere attempt not to *feel* this kind of dark emotion. It is not enough to avoid *showing* the annoyance. Bottled up aggravation can sometimes do more damage than that which is expressed. No, the best way to approach the matter is not to allow this negative coloring into the emotions at all. Think of it in allegorical terms. If the resentment and aggravation is compared to a river which starts as a small trickle high in the mountains, and gathers volume as it runs down the mountainside, it will be understood that to deliberately suppress the acting out of the negative feeling is like building a dam across the river. This will stop the flow for a while, but the river keeps on coming down the mountain, and sooner or later either the dam will burst (equivalent to losing control and erupting in a fireworks of temper, violence or anger), or the sluice gates will have to be opened to relieve the pressure (equivalent to 'working off steam' — for example, by getting one's frustration out in aggressive sports, etc.). Neither of these measures is particularly healthful, for neither one leads in the direction of dismantling the tendency to develop the feelings of frustration, annoyance and aggravation. The better way, using the allegory, is to go up the mountain to the *source* of the river, and there plug up the spring from whence the river comes. This is equivalent to so controlling one's inner state that no feeling of anger or irritation ever gets started. A counsel of perfection, some might say. And yet it is not so difficult if some effort is put into the task — and if it is approached with an understanding of how best to succeed. We will attempt here to sketch one way which may offer success to those to whom the approach we take in our books appeals. The mind is the most powerful instrument of the will, and it is through the mind that the problem can be resolved.

The first step in this procedure is to learn to generate within one's heart a feeling of *love*, and to be able to do this *at will*. By developing this wonderful ability, one arms oneself with the best defence against aggravation and irritation, for none of these negative emotions can possibly exist alongside the pure emotion

of love and affection. The procedure involves first
picturing the person whom you love the most at the
present time. Hold that picture in your mind, and
allow your heart to stream love out toward that individual. Practice holding the image and the feeling
together for one minute at a time. You will soon get
to the point where you can maintain the love vibration
for up to three minutes. When you have reached that
time-length, then while maintaining the love feeling
in your heart, turned up to maximum so-to-speak,
allow the image to switch from the loved individual to
someone of whom you are fond, though not to the same
extent as the first person. Continue to hold the love
stream flowing from your heart, and replace the second person with someone who is merely an acquain-
tance, but for whom you have not previously felt any
great love emotion. Finally – and remember that you
can accomplish this – allow the image toward which you
are streaming love to change to someone that you normally resent or dislike. When you can arrive at this
last stage, you will be in a position to beam the love
vibration at any person or any situation.

Then, when the aggravating circumstances threaten
to arise, simply turn on the love generator you have
now perfected. We guarantee that if you can beam
love at the thing, person or situation which appears
to be a source of irration, it will forthwith cease to
appear as such. All negativity in the circumstance
will simply evaporate.

We would like to assure those who have doubts
about this process that by beaming love at your enemy, you do not give the enemy more power over you.
Precisely the opposite occurs. Enmity can only exist
if it is fed by negative emotion. By cutting off your
own resentment, your erstwhile enemy can no longer
continue as such. The energy which you were previously feeding him is no longer available, and therefore the force which sustained his feeling will disappear.

Chapter 8
The Other Phalanges

In a general way, the other phalanges of the fingers also relate to life-lessons, though they are not
as important as those represented by the end phalanges. Several of the other phalanges refer to
specific manifestations of the end phalanges, as will
be seen from what follows.

Figure 9 shows all of the fingers, and identifies
the basic lessons to which the various phalanges
refer.

The middle phalange of the little finger relates to a
willingness to do menial tasks – jobs which many
might consider 'beneath them'. This can often show
up in the work situation, when a person feels that
his true worth is not being recognized, or that he is
'above' doing the kind of work he has been given.
This attitude is a stumbling block in terms of spiritual progress, and the longer one resents the menial
nature of his work, the longer (in general) he will
have that kind of work to do. Impatience and frustration at being 'held down' in this way are shown
by a particularly short middle phalange on the little
finger. We will deal with how to interpret these other
phalanges fully when we have identified and discussed
all of them.

The lowest phalange of the little finger, or L3, refers to passing judgement on others. This may be an
expressed or a silent judgement – it does not matter.
The biblical injunction, 'Judge not' is the only proper
attitude to have when confronted by situations or

people upon whom we are tempted to pass judgement. For only by refraining from judging others can we be certain that our assessment of *ourselves* is unclouded and accurate. For our powers of judgement were given to allow each of us to assess his *own* failings and errors, not those of others. This is a particularly important lesson for those born under the sign Virgo, or for those with important planets in that zodiac sign. Remember that almost no soul comes to earth without some blot, failing or lesson that needs learning. With only a handful of exceptions, every person incarnate on the earth comes in a flawed condition. If you were perfect it would be almost impossible for you to stay in your body, so vast would be the difference in vibration between your soul and the earth plane. All who come have fallen short, you included, and the intent was that each human should learn to cherish his brothers even with all their faults, nay, *because* of those faults – just as the Father in Heaven does. If *God* does not judge His earth children, what right has *man* to do so?

The finger designated as R2 (the middle phalange of the Ring Finger) has a more general meaning, for it points to the capacity to accept karmic burdens, to face up to hardship and adversity, and to shoulder with a good will the burdens which are placed upon one's back during an earth incarnation. The material plane is that in which karmic loads are discharged, in which the burdens that weigh down the soul are lightened through suffering and hardship. This concept is available to all souls at the subconscious level, and each human knows that this is the function of the earth plane. However, the current self-oriented attitude among mankind has fostered the view that life should be all 'clear sailing', that the aim of existence should be to remove aggravation at any cost, to avoid unpleasant responsibilities and to shirk the experiences which might seem irksome. And yet it is through hardship and pain that the human soul learns most quickly. Souls in the between-life stage long for a chance to come again to the earth in order to have the opportunity to set aside their karmic load, and to learn that which was neglected in previous lives.

Even without a knowledge of karma and rebirth, however, it is possible to develop an attitude which allows hardship to borne cheerfully. Within the

Christian tradition, many people will say, "well, that's a cross I had to bear", accepting the burden philosophically, albeit without a complete knowledge of what lies behind this necessity for pain and suffering.

R3 refers to the ability to accept without complaint the necessity of making do with a relatively low income. Some souls are so mesmerized by the thought of wealth, that they agonize continually over the smallness of their salary, expending great mental effort in this fruitless obsession. It represents a particular sub-category of the 'money lesson' which is more generally designated on the end phalange of the same finger.

M2 designates the lesson of patience. It is often stated as: "God's time, not man's time". Many souls have great difficulty in accepting the necessity to wait for what they want. Indeed, the flaw which they have is not so much the inability to wait, as the tendency to *want* something so badly that they be-- come impatient. The problem stems from a failure to realize that what an incarnated personality thinks is best for him is rarely what his guides and guardians consider proper for the advancement of the soul. The best approach here is simply to accept that all things have their seasons, and that if some particular thing or phase is intended to come into one's life, that will occur when the time is right from a higher perspective, and not one second before.

M3 points to the necessity – applied to numerous souls – to undergo a period in which the home surroundings are rather more humble than what the soul may think it deserves. Many individuals have, in previous lives, become used to opulence and privilege – so much so that they have developed an expectation that this should always be the case in an earth incarnation. Even worse, many such souls have concluded, on the basis of the previous opulence, that they are somehow 'better' than other people who have not been born into similar circumstances. It has been found by humanity's guides that the best way to dismantle a feeling of superiority based on opulent and privileged lives is to put the soul through certain experiences of the opposite life-pattern, to drag the individual through one or more lives in 'reduced circumstances', as the old expression has it.

69

F2 and F3 point to failings which all will understand: anger and violence, respectively. It is important to distinguish between these. Anger may or may not give an impetus to violent behavior. Violence is not always motivated by anger (thought this is usually the case). Each of these tendencies represents a particular flaw, and it is the task of each soul so afflicted to strive to rid himself of both of these very negative tendencies.

T2 points to temper. This again is to be distinguished from both anger and violence. Temper is something which erupts spontaneously, as if out of the person's control, whereas anger can simmer and brood for days or weeks without showing on the surface in terms of deliberate action. We do not need to say much further in regard to these three different aspects of negative emotion, aside from pointing out that all three have a direct bearing on the basic lesson represented by T1, namely, the ability to 'turn the other cheek'.

Having now explained the connotations of all the phalanges, it remains but to tell how these phalanges are to be read.

The best approach is to look for some sign which appears to be drawing attention to one or more particular phalanges. Such a sign may be *anything which draws your eye to it*. A scar, for example, or a wart, cut, spot, malformation, injury, etc. These signals are also to be applied to the *end* phalanges. Think of it in this way: the guides do not lose any opportunity to pass information that may be of use to a soul in terms of its spiritual pilgrimage. If an individual has been having fits of temper recently, caused perhaps by a set of circumstances that has recently arisen, then his guides may arrange for him to injure the T2 phalange – as a signal to his subconscious (which is perfectly aware of the meanings we have explained above) that he should try to overcome this failing – or indeed that this set of aggravating circumstances has been arranged precisely to give him the *opportunity* to overcome the failing of temper. If life could be looked on generally in this vein (with or without an understanding of the phalange symbology) then much improvement could be effected in situations which now tend only to cement the old bad habits through repetition.

If you find that your attention is drawn to one

particular phalange through such a signal, then it would be wise to approach the matter gently, perhaps by simply questioning the person whose hand you are reading — attempting to make him realize for himself what the signal might mean. We should emphasize that the skill we are imparting should never be looked on as a way to impress others with one's occult knowledge, but rather as an opportunity to help one's brothers along their chosen paths. Indeed, there is a law to the effect that, the more one's knowledge is used to help or comfort others, the more of that knowledge one will receive. Conversely, the more one's knowledge is used for vainglory, or to impress others, or to enrich the self to the detriment of others, the further the soul will be held away from a complete grasp of the subject.

With respect to the middle and lower phalanges of all the fingers, the 'score lines' running parallel to the fingers represent, in each case, the number of previous lives in which that particular lesson was set to be learned fully *but was not*. See Figure 10. Hence, a phalange with numerous vertical score-lines points to a lesson that has proven particularly difficult for the soul to learn, thus hinting that special effort ought to be put into learning it now. When one of the middle or lower lessons has been thoroughly learned, the respective phalange will appear without vertical score lines.

Finally we will deal with the indicator which points to particular times during the life when the various lessons will have to be faced and, hopefully, learned. On many phalanges, one will find *cross* score lines, such as those illustrated in Figure 11. The time-relation is read by considering that the life begins at the bottom of each phalange and progresses to the top, with the middle of the phalange representing age 35, give or take two years. The middle phalange in Figure 11 has been labelled to illustrate that the cross line coming in from the right hand side is located at about age 40 or so. For the bottom phalange in Figure 11 the ages are about 35 and 38. For the top phalange, the lines represent ages 20, 30 and 40, approximately.

The interpretation is relatively simple: At the age or ages indicated by the cross lines, the particular lesson designated by the phalange will 'come up for review', so to speak. The individual will be given an

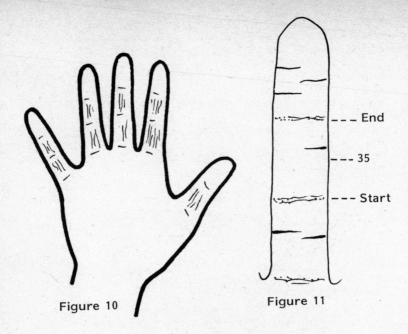

Figure 10

Figure 11

--- End

--- 35

--- Start

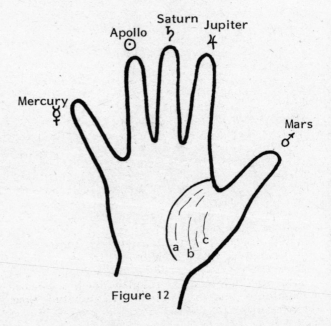

Apollo ☉

Saturn ♄

Jupiter ♃

Mercury ☿

Mars ♂

a b c

Figure 12

72

opportunity to show whether he has learned the lesson involved. If he has not, then aggravation and difficulity will arise due to this failure.

For example, if there is a cross line at the middle of M2, designating patience, then one may be reasonably certain that, at or about age 35, a set of circumstances will arise which will sorely test the person's ability to be patient, to wait. If he has learned the lesson, then the set of circumstances will not cause him trouble. If he has not, he will suffer because of it.

A special word is in order regarding the phalange R2 in terms of the cross-line testing times. For R2, any cross-line points generally to a time when some karma must be set aside through difficulty. By adopting a philosophy of the willing acceptance of burdens, by knowing that all pain serves a higher purpose (even one we do not fully understand), the trial may be lightened.

With respect to the *lengths* of the phalanges, there is a general approach which will allow a grasp of any *difference* in the length of any given phalange compared to others. According to this approach, an overly long phalange is saying that effort *has* been put into learning that particular lesson in past lives and that some progress has been made, but the learning is somehow 'wide of the mark'. A short phalange as compared to the others points to a failure to learn in the past, and particularly to an impatience and irritation with respect to the necessity of learning that specific lesson. We will give examples to illustrate both of these conditions.

Suppose a person has the end phalange of the forefinger clearly longer than the other phalanges on *that finger* (comparisons should always be made firstly with the other parts of the same finger, and only then with the rest of the finger phalanges). This will designate the area of faith in some higher reality or creative principle, and will suggest that an attitude or conclusion *has* been reached after wrestling with that particular lesson, but that somehow the individual has not arrived at the most balanced or correct point of view – seen from a spiritual perspective. An example would be the bible-thumping, 'hellfire and damnation' approach to religion which does more to frighten people than to hold up a spiritual example. Such souls have indeed come to a 'belief' in some power beyond man, but their conception of the Creator as a vengeful, dictatorial being has nothing to do with the spiritual realities of the universe. Another example of a faulty grasp of the 'faith' lesson is represented by the currently popular mohammedan view that sanctions holy wars or 'jihads' against all enemies of the moslem faith, and that believes in a god who approves of such savagery as many in the Moslem world now practice daily.

It is not necessary to give further examples for the other phalanges in terms of excessive length, as the one we have just offered will suffice.

As for the noticeably short phalange (again as compared primarily to the other phalanges of the same finger), this will designate impatience with the necessity of learning that lesson, as aforesaid. If the end phalange of the forefinger were shorter than the others, it could represent an irritation or impatience with any suggestion that there are realities beyond the world of the five senses, or some form of resentment of organized religion. There are many ways in which this could manifest, and we must leave the seeker to arrive at his own interpretation in each case.

Finally we must point out that the shortness or length of the phalanges is set at birth, and that the conditions to which these point are intended to be overcome or rectified during the life. Now, it is the case that few individuals now on the earth make rapid progress with their spiritual lessons, and therefore one should not be surprised to find that the meanings attributed above to phalanges which are different in length will apply. However, there are a good number of individuals who have, by dint of sheer effort, overcome the flaws and shortcomings with which they were born. Thus there are bound to be instances in which the above significance does not apply, due to the fact that the person has changed significantly during the present life.

Finally we would single out the kinds of hands in which certain of the fingers are seen to curve noticeably. In most such hands, one or more of the fingers will seem to be curving toward another which remains straight. This will signify the importance of the finger which is, in effect, 'drawing' the others toward it due to its influence. In order to analyze hands of this type one needs to know the planetary rulership of the fingers, which is illustrated in Figure 12. Beginning with the little finger, this is ruled by Mercury, as we have mentioned previously. As such the significance of the finger includes the sexual area, business and all communicative interchange. The ring finger is ruled by the Sun or Apollo, which governs the concept of 'personal significance'. Many people derive their personal feeling of significance from their love-bond relationship, which is why this area falls under the ring finger (and indeed, is why this finger wears the wedding ring). The middle finger is ruled by Saturn. Saturn is the planet which is directly tied to all that which limits, restricts, denies, delays and teaches lessons. Saturn in Astrology is the 'taskmaster of the zodiac' and this title also applies directly in palmistry. Lines and marks which are associated with or stem from the Saturn finger always point to areas where something of a lesson-learning or karmic nature is involved. In the east, it is understood that Saturn is the planet *par excellence* of ḳarma, a word designating the great law of cause and effect, particularly as it weaves its influence from life to life – requiring that past actions which brought pain to others be 'offset' by undergoing a similar form of pain or difficulty oneself. The middle finger rules all that which smacks of Saturn's influence in life: law and order, government, responsibility, illness, hardships generally, and the like.

The forefinger pertains to the broad question of faith generally, and is ruled by Jupiter. This planet, in astrology, is looked on as the bounteous influence in a chart, the point from which benefits flow into the life. The planet Jupiter is seen as the planet of increase, help, 'luck' (as this is popularly conceived) and the multiplying or duplicating of anything. Hence the printing industry (which produces many copies of a single item) is clearly under the rulership of the planet Jupiter. In Palmistry, lines stemming from the Jupiter finger all act as pathways along which help, increase and benefit can flow.

Finally, the thumb is under the planet Mars. As such the thumb denotes *energy*, principally the physical energy with which the body is moved. It will be understood that the failings pointed to by the nail phalange of the thumb pertain to the *misuse* of energy. Irritation and temper are but perversions of the energy flow which the body should be channelling for the good of others.

Now, when one finger remains straight between two which curve toward it, the meaning is that the lesson of the straight finger has been better or more fully learned than those of the other two fingers, and further that the energies represented by the curved fingers are actually 'twisted' or distorted in some way in the make-up of the person — probably (though not necessarily) due to the over-emphasis on the energies of the straight finger. This may seem somewhat obscure, and we will therefore give an example to show what we mean.

Suppose that an individual has, on both hands, a straight Jupiter finger toward which the Saturn (middle) finger curved. This would indicate that the Jupiterian influence in the life is stronger in a positive sense than the Saturnian. The Jupiterian energies would seem to bring benefits and positive experiences, but the somewhat distorted Saturian energies would attract the difficult side of Saturn's significance into the life pattern as well. Thus, one may find, on the one hand, the positive, upright and basically faith-oriented attitude of the person under the Jupiterian influence, while at the same time the life pattern could show more than the usual degree of hardship, delay, illness, worry or karmic influence. By not having learned to handle the Saturnian energies properly, the individual's approach to responsibilities may be to shirk or ignore them; or his response to illness and delay may be resentment or irritation, rather than a calm acceptance of the necessity for these patterns.

One more example will be given, because of the importance of this area of interpretation. Suppose that the little finger and the middle finger both curved toward a straight and overly long ring finger. Now in this instance we have also introduced the notion of having an entire finger longer than it normally would be. When this occurs, the significance is that the qualities or energies represented by that finger are overly stressed in the basic personality of the individual. The overly long ring finger points to the concept of the 'personal significance', as we have already pointed out. The individual with the elongated ring finger will typically be one who is more involved with himself than the average person, who is continually seeking ways to define, understand and underscore his own importance. The rulership of this finger by the Sun is the clue to this interpretation. Now, this pattern of self-involvement may not necessarily lead to serious problems, if the person has learned not to allow the self-absorption to affect his relationships with others in a negative way. However, few who have this trait are aware that others view them as excessively self-absorbed, and therefore they will not be able easily to rectify the behavior patterns which are causing the friction or resentment on the part of others. The extended ring finger and the over-stressing of the self which it represents, in the example we have given, will probably have been responsible for the distortions of energy which are represented by the curvature of the two adjacent fingers. The curved little finger will probably designate a failure to integrate the sexual energies, while the curved middle finger will suggest a problem with the integration of the Saturian patterns of limitation, hardship, delay and karma with which the life is saddled – both likely having been caused at least in part by the previous life patterns which resulted in the excessive self-absorption.

As an aside, we should point out that there is no 'right' length for any given finger. The seeker must simply base his judgement on his own experience – after having examined a very large number of hands in order to develop a good idea of the 'average' hand shape. Generally, however, the forefinger and the ring finger are of equal length, while the little finger ends at about the bottom of the nail phalange of the ring finger. The middle finger extends from about 1/3 to about 1/2 of a phalange beyond the tips of the two adjacent fingers.

There is but one more general area of interpretation concerning the fingers themselves, relating to the fingernails. However we wish to deal with this topic separately, and shall do so in a later chapter on the health of the body.

Chapter 9
The Mounts of Venus and Luna

We wish to define the significance of these two extremely important areas of the hand before we deal with the major and minor lines of the hand, because of the necessity of taking these mounts into consideration when interpreting many of the linear markings on the palmar surface.

The Mount of Venus is, simply, the ball of the thumb. In other words, the Mount of Venus is that part of the palm which lies 'inside' the life-line and stretches over to the bottom of T2, the second thumb phalange. This Mount has been misinterpreted in various ways by the conventional palmistry texts, for no palmists have previously realized that the major purpose of this fleshy part of the palm is to show influences which arise out of past life experiences on the earth plane. More specifically, it will be noticed that, on any Mount of Venus, there are a number of faint lines running roughly parallel with the life line L. In Figure 12, some of these lines are designated by the letters a, b, c. These faint 'reflection lifelines' are just that: they are lines representing past lives which are significant in terms of the patterns encountered in the present life. Why are they faint? Because the memories of these past lives are themselves faint as far as the conscious mind is concerned. They have their influence on the current life in progress, but they do not represent specific memories in most cases. It will also be noticed that these faint lines are not whole – i.e. they do not extend fully

from top to bottom of the Mount, as does the actual
life-line L (in most cases). The significance of this
lack of completion is interesting, for it casts light on
the make-up of the subconscious of the individual.
In order to explain this, we shall have to digress
briefly.

When it is decided which soul shall incarnate in a
foetus that has been forming during pregnancy, many
tasks must be initiated and completed before the actual
birth. Among these is the designing of the palmar
lines and the patterns at the ends of the fingers.
Another important process involves the selection of
those past life memories which will become a part of
the *subconscious* of the personality about to be formed.
The guides of the soul about to enter incarnation must
first decide which lessons are to be set for the life
that is to begin, which other souls will likely be inter-
acting with the new personality, and what karma must
be offset through hardship and suffering. When these
and related decisions have been made, the contents of
the subconscious are decided upon. It is important to
realize that not all past lives are contained in the subconscious storehouse, nor are all parts of any given
past life placed there. Only that which is significant
or important for the present life is allowed to have a
part in the subconscious. Let us be more specific.

Suppose that the individual about to be born must
pass through a relationship of marriage with another
soul, either for lesson-learning purposes or for karma,
or both. And suppose that these two souls share a
certain antipathy toward each other arising from a
specific past life in which they were mortal enemies.
Yet in another, more recent life as mother and son
they developed a strong affection for each other.
The guides of these souls would rightly fear that, if
both of these past life patterns were available to the
subconscious, the memory of the antipathy they once
felt for each other might outweigh the affection which
they subsequently developed. Therefore the guides
could well decide to suppress the 'enemy' life (in
both personalities), allowing only a memory of the
positive relationship to be present. This would then
reinforce an attraction between the individual when
they meet in the new life, and would help to ensure
that they would enter into a relationship, marriage
or whatever.

As a different example, suppose these same two

individuals had had only one major life or interaction between them — which started out with much affection and mutual trust, but which ended in bitterness between them (for whatever reason). If again the guides wished to bring these two together in a marriage relationship, it would be important to keep the memory of the bitter phase out of the subconscious, and to program in only the recollection of the happier, earlier time together.

Another factor in this process relates to the possibility of 'time-delay' programming for the subconscious. For example, if the guides wished to cause the two individual to be initially attracted together into a marriage, and then to allow the memory of the past bitter experiences to surface later in order to allow the individuals the opportunity of reconciling the old feud, then they would implant the memory of the bitter experiences as a time-delay package, which would only come into its influence at a later stage in the marriage. The triggering of the time-delay memory could be done through what is called a 'reliving'. This pattern is one which is generally understood by certain groups who have studied esoteric matters. Although there is a mistaken tendency on the part of some to assume that most if not all of life's experiences are simply relivings, it is nonetheless true that many specific patterns are deliberately arranged as a reflection of a previous life experience, usually in order to trigger some memory or attitude or reaction which it is now time to deal with and integrate.

Another way to trigger a time-delay memory is Astrologically. Many individuals are sufficiently sensitive to transits to the natal planetary positions in their birth charts that such contacts can have the effect of triggering the buried memories.

When the contact occurs between the transiting planet and the natal position, a vibration is transmitted upward from the physical through the other bodies, and this tremor will awaken the slumbering recollection if it has the same basic vibratory nature as the memory itself. For example, suppose a person had lived in ancient times when brutality was a common occurrence. And suppose that person suffered greatly due to the unthinking cruelty of another — specifically the spouse. Now, cruelty combines the nature of the planets Mars and Saturn: Mars being the pain, and Saturn being the cold

callous attitude which allows one person to inflict
pain on another. In our example, a transit of Mars
to natal Saturn, or conversely a transit of Saturn
to natal Mars, could well trigger the dormant memory of that earlier life, thus dredging up the fear
and other negative emotions which were felt then,
and giving to the person the opportunity of cleans-
ing himself of the negative residue from the painful
experience.

To return to the first of the two mounts under discussion, that of Venus, it will now be understood why
the lines parallel to the Life line (denoting past lives
of significance to the present which are stored in
the subconscious) do not all run the full length of
the mount. Only parts of those lives are stored.
The other of the two mounts – the Mount of Luna
– is the direct representative of the *subconscious,
pure and simple*. In Figure 12, this mount has been
divided by broken lines into three sections: an
upper section denoting the 'memory banks' of the
subconscious, a middle region representing the
'symbolic interpretation' area, and a lower region
which contains the 'archetypes' of the individual
and of the race as a whole. We should point out
that these divisions are somewhat arbitrary, and
that the different regions of the subconscious are
occupied with additional tasks beyond those we have
stipulated above. However, these 'jobs' are the
most important in the three sectors, and therefore
there is some justification in giving them as the
principal areas of significance.
It is clear from Figure 12 that the Mount of Luna
extends only up to the Heart line. Certain texts
define the Mount as extending further up the hand,
but they do not ascribe to this region the significance we are here stressing – that of the subconscious – akin in many ways to the 'memory' of a computer but vastly greater than any man-made physical
computer in terms of the number of 'bits' of memory it
contains. It literally holds a record in the minutest
detail of every event, circumstance and experience
through which the physical personality has passed
in the present life. Naturally, much of this material is trivial in the extreme and of no great importance to the individual. Indeed, that is why this
great wealth of minor detail is only stored in the

subconscious: it is not necessary for the *conscious* mind to have any ready access to it. But the memories are always there, and always intact. If, for example, you ever decide that you wish to 'recall' the exact number of steps in the stairs of the first house you ever lived in, you can do it easily – in one of two ways. The first is simply to deal directly with your subconscious through the use of an intermediate 'instrument' like the pendulum. The other is to access the memory through hypnosis. There are several less well known techniques which allow a direct contact with the subconscious, known to the Rosicrucians and others, but it is not necessary to give them here.

The memory location of the subconscious is like a series of pigeon-holes, where the detailed recollections are endlessly stored. Because of the 'stuff' from which the subconscious computer is actually made (not physical matter, of course), the total memory is almost infinitely great. A similar material is used to construct the marvellous astral computers which are employed by humanity's guides in determining the best birth-charts for souls about to return to incarnations, and for selecting the various experiences and karma which are to be undergone. Because of the number of 'bits' of information which these astral machines must manipulate, it is not feasible to construct them from physical matter. This could be done, but there are many reasons why it is far more preferable to make them of astral matter instead. One reason is that astral matter responds far more readily to thought, which allows repair and maintenance to be almost instantaneous.

We have digressed, but we wanted to impress upon the reader the wonderful capacity of the 'computing machine' which he has been given as his subconscious. Indeed, if only men understood the great potential which lies dormant and unused within them, they would soon begin to seek ways in which to use it more fully.

The mid-region of the subconscious, designated by the intermediate part of the Mount of Luna, is that which interprets the various symbols and signals which the life-pattern of each individual ceaselessly presents to him. Indeed, all of the symbolic information we have presented thus far in this book is *fully known* by the subconscious, which was programmed with this knowledge just after the time of birth. Let us digress again in order to explain this process of storing knowledge within the subconscious.

When a new soul is preparing for a new incarnation, and the chosen foetus is developing in its mother's womb, the first steps are taken by the soul's guides to prepare the future subconscious of the earth personality about to be projected. This is a slow procedure, and cannot be completed until after the soul has linked with the new body — which happens at or shortly after physical birth. Essentially, what the guides create is the 'machine' of the subconscious — in computer jargon, the 'hardware'. This part of the process is accomplished before the physical birth. Also attended to is the storing of certain memories from past lives (the ones which are germane to the new life about to be lived) along with the residue of talents and abilities which the soul had worked to develop in previous incarnations (e.g. music, art, manual skills) and to which it is to be allowed to have access in the new life. This can be compared to the 'built-in' programming of typical computers now available: for example the 'language' which the computer understands, the ability to read certain basic commands, etc. Also allowed into the subconscious prior to actual birth are the 'old tapes' from previous incarnations. These can be compared to computer programs, often called "software". The programs of the subconscious computer can be harmful or beneficial to the individual. If the old tape reflects an unhappy period in a prior existence, for example one in which the individual developed an inferior self-image, then the implantation of that tape will tend to produce a similar attitude in the new life. Conversely, a tape which gives a positive self-picture, for example relating to a life in which the person was honored for something or achieved a great deal, will provide the new personality with a 'head start', so to speak.

One might well wonder why the guides should insert negative 'programs' into the subconscious computer. Can any good possibly come it it? Why not program in only the good material and reject all of the negative?

The answer is simple: what the guides actually do is to *censor out* material. If they did not exercise their editing role, then the subconscious would automatically store the *entire contents of the soul's memory*, both the good and the bad. Such total storage, however, would be most unsuitable for a great many individuals, who would find themselves hampered by the many negative tapes which they themselves have created in past incarnations. There remains the question as to why the guides do not simply eliminate *all* the negative programs. The answer here is complex, but can be simplified by pointing out that the negative tapes *are a part of the soul memory*, and indeed are an integral part of the soul itself. Until those negative tapes or 'bad programs' can be rewritten internally, i.e. integrated and replaced by positive ones, the soul will never be clear of the drawback which they represent to spiritual evolution. It would be pleasant enough to live an incarnation free of these negative programs, but at the end of the life nothing of positive benefit would have been achieved *for the soul*. The old tapes would still be there in the soul's make-up, and their negative influence would still be just as strong. That is why each incarnation is approached as an opportunity, not only to learn spiritual lessons and to set aside karma, but also to re-program the old tapes from prior lives which continue to act as shackles for the soul until they are erased. And the fastest way to deal with these negative programs is to come back down into incarnation on the earth – the same place where they were first created – and to positively strive to correct or rewrite them. In fact, for most of the tapes of which we are speaking this represents the *only* way it can be done – mainly because the nature of the material on the tapes pertains only to the earth plane and has no direct interpretation at higher levels of the soul's awareness.

To summarize, we may say that the guides allow into the subconscious those negative tapes which might reasonably be attended to and rewritten in the new life, but do not charge up the subconscious with so much negativity that the progress of the earth incarnation will be hampered. There is a law to the effect that no soul must be given tasks beyond its ability while in incarnation: the corollary to which is that no problem is ever so great that it cannot be solved, and no pain ever so bad that it cannot be borne. It would be well for all souls, and especially those on the path, to bear this thought always in mind.

We have yet to explain the phase in which the *symbolic* knowledge of the subconscious is entered into the memory of the 'computer'. While it might be thought that this procedure too could be attended to during the nine month gestation period, such is not the case. The matter of understanding *with the heart center* the great laws of reality cannot be 'programmed in' until the soul is fully connected to the body, and thus to the subconscious apparatus which it is being given for the duration of its new incarnation (to replace its own 'soul memory' until at death it regains access to that much more complete storage of recall). Because the symbolic understanding represents a level of comprehension which a simple computer cannot fully absorb, it is essential that the soul itself be present and have a hand in the programming of the material. In a sense, the soul's own grasp of spiritual truth must act as a guide during the programming operation, or else the interpretation of the symbols and signals during the life will not be fully understood by the individual. This concept will become clear presently.

Let us assume that a foetus is about to be born, and that the intended soul is standing by, awaiting the 'operation' which will tie it to the new body. After the connection has been made, which requires a certain severance between the soul and its own memory, the soul has temporarily forgotten many of the great laws and truths that form part of the spiritual teaching it has been assimilating throughout its incarnational experience. During the first nine months of life after birth, the soul leaves the body during sleep and travels back to the astral levels from whence it has recently come, there to attend schools in which it learns many things – including the symbolic interpretive information which is to be added to the subconscious computer. Only by having the soul itself go through the learning process can it be ensured that the subconscious will store the data correctly and in a manner most understandable to the conscious mind which is gradually developing.

We might digress here to point out that the reason for the fontanelle of a newborn (the soft portion at the top of the skull, where the skull bones have not yet come together) is to allow the soul to escape readily from the body and to return to the astral schools during the first few months of life. Indeed, many people who remark on how beautiful or 'at peace' a sleeping infant looks might be interested to know that it is because the soul is once again in its between-life state – one of far more joy and bliss than can be found on the earth – and is there learning from the lips of great master souls the eternal truths of God's creation.

Finally we come to the lowermost part of the Mount of Luna, which denotes the region where live the personal and racial archetypes. The concept of archetypes will not be strange to many readers although it is difficult to define succinctly just what they are. Basically, an archetype is a pattern or symbol which contains within itself a complete thought, principle or *gestalt* that incorporates a building block in the understanding of the soul. "Perfection", for example, is a notion which individuals will interpret differently, and for which different people will have different corresponding archetypes. For some the archetype may be a noble metal like gold or silver. For others, perfection may be represented by a number, or the shape of a circle, or the sound of the perfect fifth in music. In many cases, the archetypes are commonly held by most if not all human beings. For example, the dragon of myth and legend generally represents the embodiment of evil or the destructive and involutionary forces. The snake on the other hand can represent either great wisdom or something of a negative nature, depending upon the individual involved.

These, then, are archetypes – and all of them dwell in the deepest depths of the subconscious: that represented by the lowest part of the Mount of Luna.

These three regions on the Mount of Luna will assume greater significance as we proceed further with our explanation of the hand lines.

The markings on the Mount of Luna always denote subconscious contents or attitudes which strongly influence the conscious personality, whether the latter realizes it or not. We will give a few examples.

A few individuals are found to have whorl or loop patterns on the Mount of Luna, similar in shape to

the whorls and loops at the ends of the fingers.
These markings always denote an *increased sensitivity* – either to outside influences, to one's own
inner states or simply to any input. The whorl
shows heightened sensitivity in a general way,
without stipulating the area which has the greatest
influence. The loop which opens outwardly toward
the edge of the hand shows sensitivity to outside
influences (usually to other people). This is shown
at P in Figure 12. The loop which opens inwardly
of the hand (shown at Q) denotes a heightened
sensitivity to *internal* states, and can denote one
who is overly self-absorbed. In many instances
this inwardly opening loop is directly connected
with the end of the Head line (H), which suggests
that the individual tends to *think* too much about
the self, to turn over in the mind ceaselessly certain aspects of its own experience which might be
better left alone. Many souls waste prodigious energy, especially mental energy, thinking about
things that are either unworthy of their attention,
or not conducive to the improvement of the inner
attributes. Endless preoccupation with one's looks
is a good example. Few activities are as much a
waste of time as this one. Yet more than half of all
souls in incarnation are caught up on some preoccupation having to do with their physical appearance.
We might say that an excellent exercise for anyone
seeking a more 'in-tune' relation with the universe
is to try to isolate their own particular area of self-
absorption, and to delete the habit from their daily
routine.

Returning to the markings on the Mount of Luna,
we would point out that any noticeable scar shows
that the person is carrying around a memory which
is 'scarring' the soul in some manner. If such a
person could isolate the memory and 'overwrite' it
with something more positive, then a considerable
benefit would result at the higher or soul level.

Warts, discolorations, and other markings all have
their tales to tell. However, the specific significance will vary for the same mark from individual to
individual. The seeker should simply rely upon his
own intuition to give him the appropriate interpretation for any who ask him to interpret the signs on
their hands.

Chapter 10
The Major Lines

We have already pointed out that the three major palmar lines – the Head, Heart and Life lines – represent directly the three main facets of the human being: the capacity to think, the capacity to love and the capacity to act. The first pertains to the intellect or mind; the second pertains to the heart side or affections; the third pertains to the body itself. In connection with the latter, the relevant side of the human 'triangle' relates not only to the body *per se*, but also to the body as the instrument of *will* and the *creative urges*. In the analog of the Christian Trinity, God the Father corresponds to the body/will/creativity, while God the Son corresponds to the love facet. God the Holy Ghost then pertains to the mental facet of man.

The three major lines show not only the general nature of the particular facet being designated, but also the sequence of major preplanned events and circumstances which have been arranged to touch the individual in that particular area. In connection with the latter concept, the course of the life is read *along the line*, always beginning with the thickest part of the line and moving toward the thinnest portion. This general law has almost no exceptions in palmistry. We are aware that many text books teach the opposite notion in regard to the Heart line, maintaining that the passage of time is read from under the forefinger toward the percussion (toward the little finger). However, we hope

to demonstrate conclusively that, using the system
we are about to set forth, the best directionality
to use is that from the thick end to the thin end of
any line.

Before dealing with the reading of specific events
on the major lines, we wish to explain the ultimately
more important area of deducing general characteristics from these lines.

The main thing to bear in mind always, when
attempting to interpret the palm, is that the beings
who mark the palm for you to read *do not mean the
matter to be difficult or obscure*. Indeed, within
the limitations and strictures that have been decreed for palmistry, the entities who design the
palmar pattern always strive to make the reading
of the palm as straightforward as possible. Think
of it in these terms: palmistry as a means for passing information is intended to be as useful and as
complete as possible, given the strictures which
apply. No entity responsible for designing the
hand of a human being would ever attempt to make
the matter of interpretation anything but the *simplest* possible. Palmistry is not an exercise in decoding obscure symbols; it is not meant to be a 'chal-
lenge' or a difficulty. Its whole purpose is to pass
along information that could be of use to the individual whose hands are being read, and therefore it
must be made as simple as possible.

But what of the strictures we have mentioned?
Why apply any limitations at all, one might ask?
Why not use letters or numbers instead of lines and
creases, since these would be even easier to read.

The explanation for the strictures is simple.
Man is now in an age of unbelief. If the palmar
markings were made too clear, and if even the
skeptics could see plainly that the hand markings
carried a direct outline of the events of the life and
a general portrait of the individual, then they would
be forced out of their skepticism regarding higher
truths and higher planes. But such forcing of the
skeptic must not occur. Any who wish to cling to
a conviction that physical life is all there is, or that
existence has no deeper meaning than the pleasure
of the moment or the grabbing of as much money or
wealth as possible before death – *must be allowed
to maintain that view*. Think of it in prosaic terms,
in connection with the raising of children. If a

child is made to "be good" merely by the continual threat of physical punishment for doing wrong, then what has been gained by the child apart from a fear complex and probably a resentment or hatred of the disciplinarian parent? The decision to act correctly or honestly or whatever has not arisen *from within the child*, and since habits of right action or thought become an integral part of the higher self only when the decision to adopt them comes from the free will decision of the individual, the fear-based reaction of the child which prompts him to proper conduct will be a part of the earth personality only. It is far better to set up circumstances for the child in which it *chooses freely and uncoerced* to act properly. We are not saying that the child should be simply left to choose on its own. The setting of proper models by the parents, the constant demonstration of love and support for the child, and the establishment of a consistent pattern of consequences for any actions of which the parents disapprove, will work wonders in the training of any child. The reference to consequences does not include physical punishment or the showing of anger toward the child: the parent merely explains to the child in a gentle and loving manner why the particular action is not acceptable, further explains that every time the child does the disapproved-of action, the particular consequence will follow, and then leaves the decision entirely up to the child. It is important to persuade the child that he can continue to do the wrong action without angering the parent, so long as it is understood that the particular consequence will follow. That way, the child does not feel that he is being coerced, he sees his free will intact, and he knows that the parent will not be angry with him. So long as the consequence is consistently presented for each infraction, the child will eventually decide to give up the offending action. And that decision will affect not only the physical personality, but the higher self as well.

We do not have time to explain this system of child-rearing further, nor is it necessary since the idea has already been impressed upon an author who has provided the teaching in book form. We have asked this channel to give details of the book at the bottom of this page, for any who may be interested.

As often happens in these books, we have again digressed. However, we wanted to sketch this excellent system of child training in this book as we do not expect to be able to write again at any length through this channel for at least several years. And of course we also wished to present a practical example showing why coercing *any* activity or belief is actually counter-productive in the long run. It is for this reason that the science of palmistry requires not only training but also a belief that some information of value is being conveyed in the lines and other markings of the hand. If the subject were to be made transparently obvious for any person, regardless of his belief system, then those who have rejected the concept of God, or who have turned their backs upon the notion of higher realms, would not be able to retain that attitude. And God wishes each one of His earth children to be free – totally free – free even to reject Him if they wish. Is any greater love even conceivable?

So it is too with the subject of Astrology. The patterns of meaning must not be made too obvious – again to allow the rational doubters and skeptics to retain their positions. In the case of Astrology, the development of man's rational ability has made it necessary to obscure certain meanings that formerly would have been used consistently. For example, it often happens that a transit to a major natal planet will occur without any event or circumstance of equivalent vibration taking place in the life. Some schools deal with these apparent 'misses' by saying that the effect is only on the inner planes, however this avoids the problem – for in other cases the transits do coincide with clear life-patterns that are definitely indicated by the planetary significances. What has happened is that a decree was passed down to the effect that major life-events should coincide wherever possible with *some* con-

*Parent's Handbook, Systemic Training for Effective Parenting, by Don Dinkmeyer PhD. and Gary D. McKay PhD.; published by American Guidance Service Inc., Circle Pines, Minn., USA, 55014

tact between natal and 'progressing' planets, but that the straight transits were not always to be used. Instead, the so-called secondaries (progressions) and the tertiaries (one ephermeris day equals one lunar month of the life) were to be made use of. It was feared that, with the advent of computers and the spread of the knowledge of mathematics, it would be too easy to persuade oneself intellectually of the truth of astrology. The doubters and skeptics would find themselves coerced by the evidence of their own calculations into abandoning their philosophical stance.

But it was not desired that any human being be coerced. Faith in a higher purpose must rise up from the well-springs of certainty within the heart center, or else not at all. Indeed, any who believe in a greater concept of the purpose of life *must* do so on the basis of an *inner* conviction, or else the persuasion is doomed to be only temporary. The higher self will not accept a belief which is supported only by the mind. The heart too must know, or else it is not truth to the soul.

Even the events of what we have called the Tribulation – a period of seven years during which upheaval and war will bring down the curtain on the world-system as it now is – must be susceptible of 'natural' interpretations, to allow the skeptics to remain hardened to the end, if they so choose. To have miraculous signs appearing in the sky, or to arrange too literal a playing out of the events foreshadowed in the Revelations, would force belief on the earth personalities only, while the higher selves of the skeptics would remain untouched by the fear-prompted 'conversion'. No, the acceptance of God, or of Christ, or of the truths of the spirit, must arise from within the heart, for in no other way will the soul take a step forward in its evolution.

We now wish to return to the question which launched the digression just terminated: how to look upon the matter of interpreting the markings of the hand? Again we emphasize that the best approach is to assume that the entities responsible for designing the hand you are attempting to read did not wish to confuse you, nor to make the interpretation difficult or obscure. While always staying within the decree to design the hand in such a way that a skeptic can reject the notion of meaning, they are to cram as much clearly readable information as possible into the design.

Always remember too that your own guides and helpers are never far away when you are attempting to help any other soul — whether it be through palmistry or in any other way. Your guides are quite expert at interpreting palms, and moreover have the advantage of being able to consult with the guides of the person you are trying to help. Armed with this extra information and their higher perspective, they are in a position to impress upon your awareness the best approach to meaning that can be taken for that person at that time. Simply open yourself up to the impressions which they are trying to pass to you, and when you hit upon something, say it. No matter that the rational intellect rejects the interpretation as unlikely or far-fetched. Indeed, the more far-fetched it seems, the more likely is it that it has come from your own guides. Hence the more likely that it is correct.

One might well ask, well if my guides can interpret the hands for me, why do I need to study any book? The answer is, of course, that your guides can only impress you with thoughts that fall within the categories of meaning that you normally entertain. The main purpose of this book, as with all of our earlier books, is to broaden the horizons of meaning in the reader's mind. Specifically, this discussion of palmistry is meant to open the mind of the reader to the wonderful possibilities of significance which the hand *can* convey, in order to allow your guides a greater latitude when they attempt to impress thoughts upon your conscious mind. Moreover, the more you understand of palmistry, the more your guides can embellish your understanding from their level.

Let us now turn to the major lines, dealing first with the Heart line.

The Heart Line

The general rule to apply when interpreting any of the major lines in terms of the general characteristics of the individual is this: examine carefully the words you would use to describe the lines, and then use those words or similar ones to describe

the characteristics. For example, a Heart line that
twists and turns rather than going straight from its
commencement under Mercury (the Mercury or
little finger) to its termination under Saturn or
Jupiter is pointing to a love nature which itself is
marked by 'twists and turns'. The individual finds
that his love experience is pulled here and there,
that he has difficulty ploughing straight ahead in
his love experiences. We will begin by showing
and describing the 'ideal' Heart line. In Figure 13,
the model Heart line commences under Mercury,
and proceeds clean and clear in a smooth curve to
end at the middle of the Jupiter finger. This represents an affectional nature which has passed all
tests and learned all lessons, a love that ask nothing back but gives all out. The affection is not
conditional, it is not trammelled by notions of sexuality, nor does it require any mental stimulation
from the loved one in order to keep it going. The
affection floods from the heart as a river pouring
to the sea: kind, generous, sincere and open.

How many can say that this describes their love
nature?

Few indeed. And just as rare is the appearance
of the 'perfect' Heart line which we have drawn in
Figure 13. Virtually every human soul now upon
the earth has a Heart line which includes some de-
parture from the ideal line drawn in the Figure.
The nature of the divergence tells clearly the shortcomings in the love nature which have yet to be
dealt with – the lessons yet to be learned.

We will discuss first the matter of the termination
of the Heart line. Having pointed out that the
ideal termination is midway of the Jupiter base, it
will be evident that any other ending for this line
represents a falling short of the perfection that is
desired. In a general way we can distinguish between Heart lines which end under Jupiter (whether
touching its base or not) and Heart lines which end
under Saturn. Jupiter is positive, benefic, generous and grand. Saturn is negative, malefic, niggardly and closed. Saturn pertains to all that
which limits man while in earth incarnation: illness,
constraint, sorrow and karma. When a heart line
ends in the vicinity of the Jupiter finger as in
Fig. 14, the significance is that there is present
a clear potential for open, loving actions and feel-

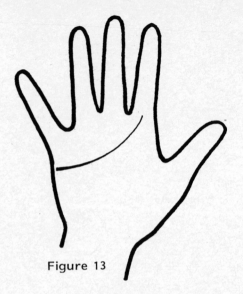

Figure 13

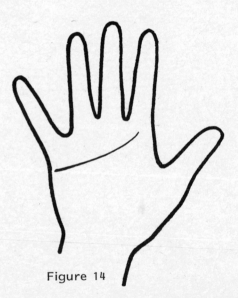

Figure 14

ings. The heart center is less closed or bottled up than when the termination is under Saturn, as in Fig. 15. In the latter case, the Saturnian influence is pointing to some constraint, coldness or pain in the heart facet which has likely caused a closing off of the affectional urges. If the Heart line merely ends under Saturn without turning up to point at the middle finger, a general indicator of a closed nature is being signalled. The cause of the difficulty may be found either in the present or in a past life. However, when the Heart line actually bends upwardly and terminates at the base of Saturn (Fig. 16), then the meaning is usually that events in the present life have strongly influenced the love nature of the individual in a negative way. In many cases, an absence of love and affectional demonstration in the early home has resulted in an inability to show warmth spontaneously to others. Sometimes the difficulty in the early home merely adds to characteristics which were brought forward from past lives, and cements them into a permanent attitude of wariness and a walled-in approach to love and affection.

In order to understand the meaning of other termination patterns for the Heart line, we must briefly describe the Head line and the Girdle of Venus. The basic significance of the Head line has already been pointed out: namely the mental and intellectual side of the human being. The Girdle of Venus is usually a complete or incomplete ring which normally stretches from the junction of Mercury and Apollo to the junction of Saturn and Jupiter. Although we have referred to the Girdle as a ring, it is easier to think of it as being made up of two separate parts: a first line extending inward at an angle from the joint between Mercury and Apollo, and a second line extending the other way obliquely from the joint between Saturn and Jupiter. See Figure 17, parts A and B. The significance of the Girdle of Venus is essentially that of the sexual drives of the personality. The differentiation between the two component lines is this: the line A originating between Saturn and Jupiter denotes the contribution to sexuality from the higher self or soul — i.e. the habits of expectation and action regarding the sexual nature which derive from experiences and patterns in past lives and which have

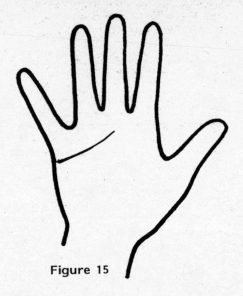

Figure 15

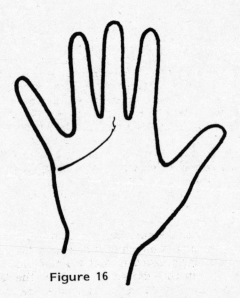

Figure 16

become a part of the soul's normal vibration; the line B originating between Mercury and Apollo denotes that portion of the sexuality which comes from the present life and the genetic inheritance of the body.

Now when the Heart line links up with the Saturn/Jupiter part of the Girdle of Venus, as shown in Figure 18, the meaning is simply that the love nature – the ability to allow pure affection to manifest – is bound up with the sexuality to such a degree that *physical* and 'chemistry' vibrations may play too important a role in determining a partner. This may surface, in mild cases, merely as a tendency to stress the *looks* of the partner above internal qualities when making the selection of a mate. In extreme cases, one finds that the sexual nature runs rough-shod over the pure affectional impulses, and drag the individual into relationships based solely upon the sexual compatibility of the two partners. And of course, any relationship based solely upon sex is doomed ultimately to failure. We have pointed out in our earlier books that sex alone cannot keep the flame of a relationship burning, when intellectual stimulation is lacking or when the purer light of true love and affection is not present. Man consists of the three facets we have described earlier, and unless his affectional relationships can also partake of this triple manifestation of the divine in man, they must at last come to nought.

When the Heart line shows a termination which seems to be bending down toward the Head line (Fig. 19), like a dowsing branch being drawn down by the presence of water, then the significance is that the 'head is leading the heart', to use the old expression. Such people have a tendency to think too much about their relationships, and to allow rational arguments to sway their choices. They can think themselves into a relationship and then keep on thinking themselves right out of it. The question of "whether to or not" is surrounded by too many intellectual reasons, and the heart is never allowed to have its say by itself.

When one finds a Heart line which has several branching terminations which fall into different categories, the significance is that the individual has a clear choice in this life as to which of the 'endings' he will choose. For example, suppose a person has

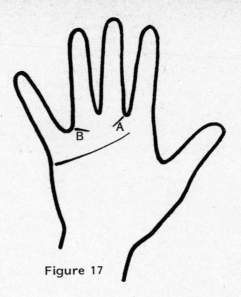

Figure 17

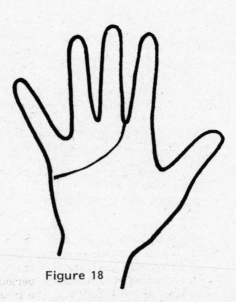

Figure 18

100

a Heart line which branches in two directions: one ending being drawn down toward the Head line, the other bending up to join one part of the Girdle of Venus. See Figure 20. In such a case, the choice is between a) allowing the head (rationality) to rule the affectional life, and b) giving in to the physical and 'chemistry' persuasions in terms of a partner. In truth, neither of these ways is the ideal. The love nature should respond to the partner merely for its own reasons, for the heart knows when another is 'right' for it. But many others can arouse the physical response known as the sexual 'chemistry' between two persons, and one can always find loads of reasons of an intellectual kind for selecting a partner: money, position, and so forth. It is unfortunate that the current life-style has persuaded so many individuals to make the selection of a partner on these fraudulent grounds, for the cloud of sorrow hangs over any relationship which is not founded on the sure heart-knowledge that the other person is 'right'.

In terms of the general nature of the Heart line, we wish to mention its straightness, the presence of islands, breaks in the Heart line, and a duplication or triplication of the line.

Straightness is a trait of the intellect. It is the mind which is able to draw a straight line. If the Heart line is presented as a straight or nearly straight line (Fig. 21), without any curvature either upwardly or downwardly, then the significance is that the mind, the intellect, is a predominating factor in the make-up of the individual. This is not to say that affection is not present, merely that it tends to take a back seat to the mind. Nor is this indicator the same as having the Heart line drawn down in a curve toward the Head line. We suggest that the previous description of a downwardly drooping Heart line be re-read and compared with what we have just said about a rectilinear Heart line.

The presence of islands or scratched-up areas on the Heart line is typically found near its commencement. See Figure 22. These confusing irregularities merely point to the 'confused' state of the individual's approach to love and affection for the period of the life corresponding to the location or the irregularities. If (as usually happens) the islands and other irregu-

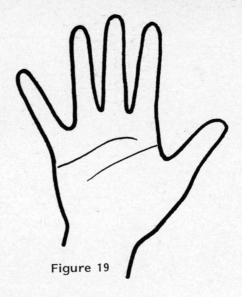

Figure 19

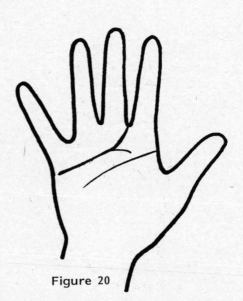

Figure 20

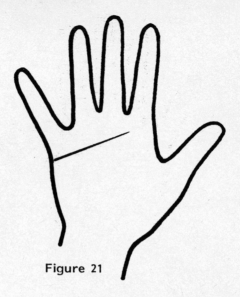

Figure 21

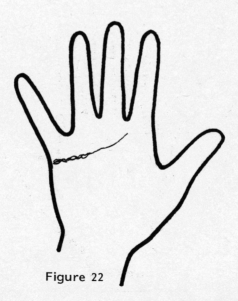

Figure 22

lar marks are bunched mainly toward the beginning of the line – under Mercury and Apollo – then they simply represent the 'searching' phase of early development for the heart center.

Often, islandings will produce double and triple lines in the Heart line for short distances, as in Figure 23. Whenever there are more than one Heart line paths, it is a clear indication that there was some duplication in the affections themselves. Either two or more relationships were being carried on, or the possibility of two was being entertained. Such a region on the Heart line denotes a time of great opportunity – a chance to learn how to bring the different facets of the love nature (physical, emotional and mental) together into one place, so that a partner can be selected with whom one can interact at all three levels.

Finally we have the matter of breaks in the Heart line. See Figure 24. This almost inevitably points to a major shake-up in the affectional life at about the time-coordinate of the separation in the line. Also, particularly when the broken heart line appears on the writing hand, there is indicated a possibility of heart attack. We say this with caution, however, since there are steps which any individual can take to protect himself from heart attack, even when such a mark is present on the writing hand. We refer to the adopting of a meatless diet and the avoidance of rich foods, smoking and drinking. So long as heart damage has not become a fact, and if the body is not too old, such protective measures are usually effective.

When the broken heart line is found in the non-writing hand, it is an indicator that a recent life (usually the most recent) ended in a heart attack or heart disease of some kind.

We now wish to give the timing coordinates by which to measure the passage of the life on the heart line. If one closes the fingers together and draws a straight line down between Mercury and Apollo parallel to those fingers, the hypothetical line will cross the Heart line at age 22, give or take a year. See Figure 25. If a further straight line is drawn down from between Saturn and Jupiter, parallel to those fingers, that hypothetical line will cross the Heart line at about age 32, give or take one year (Fig. 25). Now, this timing operates

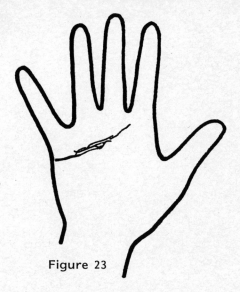

Figure 23

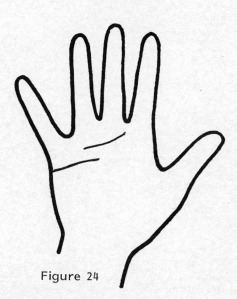

Figure 24

reliably only up to about age 32 or so. In other words, when the Heart line passes under Saturn and Jupiter the timing is not regular any more. Events affecting the affectional life must be timed from other indicators on the hand.

The main indicators of events for the Heart line are the 'influence lines' which descend from under Appollo and actually *touch* the Heart line. As a general rule, these influence lines are relationships with others of the opposite sex, which are karmically prepared from before birth. If no such lines are visible (such as those shown as examples in Figure 26), it does not mean that the life is to be devoid of relationships of an affectional kind. It merely signifies that the guides did not wish to pre-program any karmic ties of this kind into the hand. In some cases the love life is left totally free with little planned at all.

Figure 27 shows two examples of typical influence lines. The influence line A meets the Heart line at about age 20, and if one thinks of the 'flow' of the influence line as running downwardly while the Heart line flows from its commencement to its termination, it will be understood that these two flows are running at angles whch cause them to oppose each other. If two actual rivers were to meet at such a junction, then the result would be agitation and turmoil in the waters. This adverse angulation between the influence line and the Heart line is meant to show that the relationship signified by the influence line is marked by difficulty for the person whose hand is being read. It is *hard* for the person to deal with the energies of the relationship.

Conversely, the influence line B runs in a convergent way into the mainstream of the Heart line. The 'waters' of the two streams here blend smoothly because of the complementing angulation. Likewise, the relationship signified by the influence line B will be considerably more smooth and 'easy' for the person whose hand bears this mark.

We should point out that the influence line must actually contact the Heart line in order to ensure that the relationship was a real possibility. Even in cases of actual contact between the lines, however, the palm reader must be wary: the potential relationship may have presented itself at the indicated time, but one or both partners may have

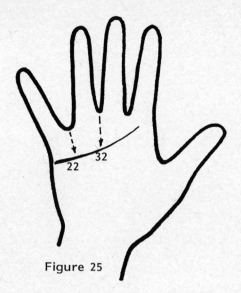

Figure 25

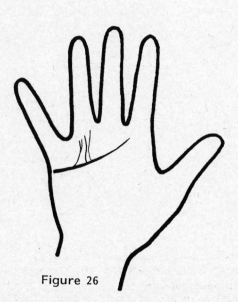

Figure 26

chosen not to enter into it. This is quite rare, but it occasionally happens. The operation of human free will is always a factor.

Figure 28 displays a common pattern: one in which a third line – a hypotenuse – stretches from the influence line A to a later point on the Heart line. The Hypotenuse (marked C) forms a triangle with the other two, and always indicates a time of 'rough waters' and testing of the relationship represented by the influence line (A) from which it extends. It cannot be said for a certainty that the relationship will break up at the contact point between C and the Heart line, although that does happen in about 70% of cases at the present time. We expect this percentage to drop dramatically in the New Age, but currently the figure remains discouragingly high. Figure 29 shows a little-understood line in association with a relationship or influence line A. The line is marked D and can be seen angling upward away from the percussion (the edge of the hand under Mercury) to touch the Heart line at about the same location as the contact between the influence line A and the Heart line. The longer the line D, the stronger are these pressures. Let us give an example. It often happens that a marriage is promoted by one's parents, with much pressure and urging on their part. Or, a person might be drawn into a marriage simply because he thinks that he is 'getting old' and the chance might not come again. These represent reasons which are not of the heart itself, and therefore fall within the category which the little line D represents.

Sometimes the line D is longer, reaching down into the region of the subconscious, as shown in Figure 30. In this case, the line D again represents incentives and pressures which are not of the Heart alone: specifically, the pressures to enter a marriage-like relationship arise due to the *memories* from past incarnations that are contained in the subconscious, and which link the person whose hand is being read with the one designated by the influence line A. In certain cases, an example being shown in Figure 31, the subconscious line D appears to sweep in a smooth curve right through the Heart line, turning into the influence line. This unification of the influence line A with the subconscious line D simply points to the great strength of the

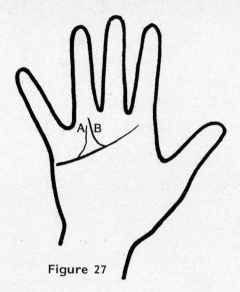

Figure 27

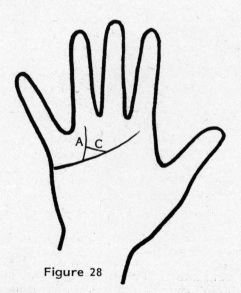

Figure 28

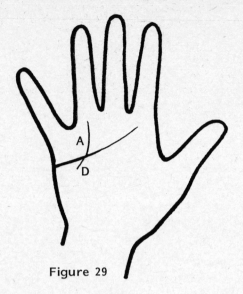

Figure 29

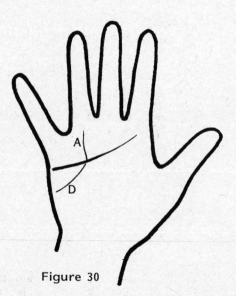

Figure 30

110

prompting to marriage which this represents. Again, however, we must remind the reader that man's will is free, and that proffered relationships may not be chosen.

We do not wish to go further into detail in regard to this fascinating area of discovery in palmistry. We will simply remind the reader to look to his intuition when attempting to interpret a hand, remembering that the guides had no wish to hide the significance from him.

The Head Line

We have already touched upon the major significance of this important line, namely its association with the mental facet of the human being. Many individuals think that the *length* of the head line is directly related to cleverness or I.Q., but this is not so. The length of the Head line relates to the *degree of importance* which the individual attaches to his mental or intellectual life, not to how clever or brainy he may be. Indeed, many souls are now in incarnation upon the earth who have a lower than average intellect, but who nonetheless stress and value the mental experiences far more highly than the physical or emotional ones. Some of this group are undergoing a karmically arranged *denial* of superior mental ability, in order to allow them to dismantle the very overemphasis which the long Head line denotes. In a previous life, such individuals may well have had an above-average intellect, but when this has led to neglect of the affectional response to others, a decision might be made to put the soul through an incarnation of limited mental capacity. However this pattern in the present may not by itself cause the person to shift his emphasis. Hence the long Head line on one who is not inordinately intelligent. By the same token, a short Head line does not betoken a small mental capacity. Many great scientists have short Head lines. The meaning in such cases is simply that, although very intelligent, such individuals have not made the mistake of overemphasizing the intellect to the neglect of the other facets of the human being.

The characteristic of the Head line which shows the nature of the mental capacity is the shape of the line itself. Look carefully at the Head line –

111

determine whether it is clearly drawn and relatively
straight, or whether it is faint, irregular or broken.
These patterns tell much more about the mind than
the length of the line. A broken Head line indicates
a period of mental stress and difficulty. An island
shows a pulling apart of the mind as it seeks to integrate or balance or choose between two competing
possibilities. The main timing indicator on the Head
line itself is its crossing with the Fate line – shown
in Figure 32. This crossing point represents about
age 30, give or take two years. It is interesting
that this age span from 28 to 32 also corresponds
with the time of the first Saturn return in Astrology,
when the planet Saturn comes back to the same location in the sky that it occupied at the individual's
birth. Astrologers well know that this return often
marks a critical time for karma and lesson testing.
The same interpretation can be applied to the
crossing of Fate and Head in palmistry. The Fate
line is essentially a Saturn line, since the way to
select the Fate line from among several candidates
is to find the one which most obviously points to
the Saturn finger. Hence, the crossing of Saturn's
line with the line of the mental life will produce a
time when karma and lessons can be brought to
bear upon the individual.

The main characteristic of the Head line which we
wish to discuss here is the slope of the line. Generally, the slope of the Head line is related to the
balance of pessimism/optimism – positive/negative –
which marks the mental outlook. Some individuals
always look on the dark side of life; they are dog-
ged by melancholy and depression. Others constantly smile, are cheerful and exhuberant, allow
the sun to smile in their faces. These two extremes
are shown by the extremes of *slope* of the Head line.

Figure 33 portrays an 'uplifted' Head line, and
denotes a similarly happy or cheerful mental disposition. Figure 34 shows the opposite: one who
is subject to melancholy or depressing thoughts
and attitudes. We must stress that the owner of
the depressive hand need not give in to the stresses
which he feels. It is possible to resist the temptation to allow the mind to slip into despond and negativity, but positive effort is required to do this.
For those who find the key which allows them to
resist the negative tendancy, there will usually ap-

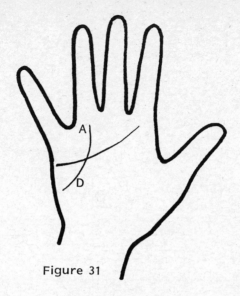

Figure 31

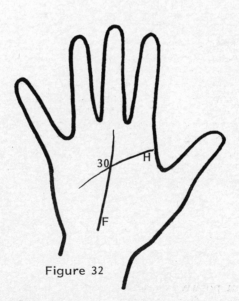

Figure 32

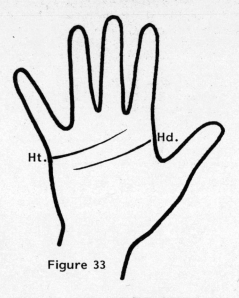

Figure 33

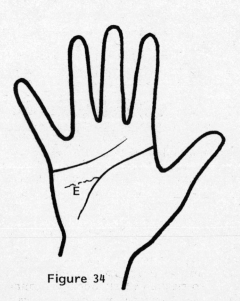

Figure 34

pear an 'escape valve' line such as is drawn at E in Figure 34, this being typically fainter than the main Head line, but representing an alternative Head line pathway nonetheless.

Figures 35, 36 and 37 show Head lines which are 'tapping in' to the subconscious of the individual at various levels. In Figure 35, the Head line contacts the subconscious in the 'pigeon-hole' region of the latter, thus allowing the mind to have ready access to this wonderful storehouse of memory. Often, as in Figure 35, the Head line must go through an S-curve in order to touch the subconscious region in the memory location just under the Heart line. The owner of a hand such as this not only generally has a positive mental disposition, but is also in a position to use this extra memory capacity for work that requires great attention to detail, the ready recall of facts and figures, and the manipulation of mathematical steps. The cashier and the bookkeeper might equally have such a mark in their hands. The signal does not point to a particular cleverness or its absence – it merely denotes an ability to tap the subconscious storehouse of memory.

Figure 36 shows a Head line which taps into the subconscious at the middle region – that pertaining to the meaning of symbolic material. The mental nature thus signalled is one which can unravel life's meaning readily, if ever given the opportunity. We stress that, in many people, this symbolic interpretive power lies dormant – because such people are not persuaded that the events and details of life hide any significance beyond the obvious. If more souls could understand that pages of meaning can be read in each 'chance encounter', that almost nothing happens that is not carefully orchestrated for the improvement and evolution of human souls, then far more would begin to utilize this magnificent 'decoding' ability which is their birthright.

Finally, Figure 37 shows a Head line which dips down deep into the lowest part of the subconscious: into that region where the archetypes dwell. A Head line such as this represents a pathway along which these strange and sometimes disturbing pictures and energies can gain access unbidden to the conscious mind. It is for this reason that many (though by no means all) suicides are found to have some form of ending or tap-root from the Head

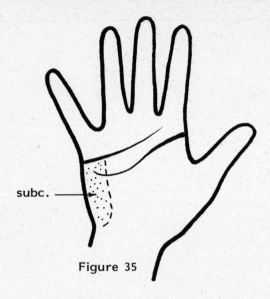

subc.

Figure 35

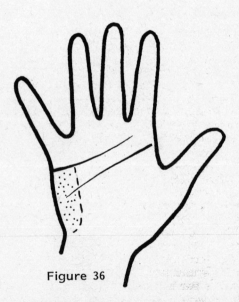

Figure 36

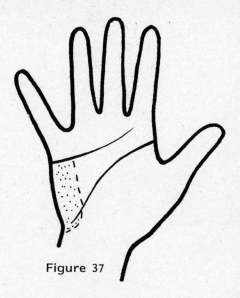

Figure 37

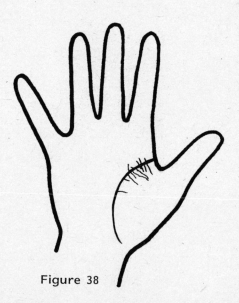

Figure 38

line reaching down into this dark abode. But at the same time, it will be found that numerous artists and creative people will also have such tap-roots into the deep subconscious. The distinction between these groups of people is a question of how the individual makes use of the material coming up along the pathway. If the individual is inherently fearful and self-absorbed, these strange and brooding energies may fill him with thoughts of darkness and self-destruction. On the other hand, if the person can learn to transform these energies into clear symbols and work with them creatively, he has the opportunity of presenting truly moving works of art to his brothers – whether these be in music, writing, the plastic arts, or whatever.

It will now be clear that sudden changes of direction in the slope of the Head line will signal an equivalent change in the mental outlook of the individual at the age indicated. Note, however, that many Head lines will be found to *gradually* deepen their slope as they proceed across the hand. Unless the direction changes dramatically, it is best simply to assume that the slowly increasing slope in the line represents the sobering effect of growing older: the dreams of youthful confidence give way to a realization that perhaps the world cannot be conquered by age 30 after all, and a more serious frame of mind become the habitual one.

The Life Line

This line is one of the most commonly misinterpreted of the lines on the hand, and at the same time it is the one about which the most people are curious. There is a misconception regarding the length of the life line which we wish primarily to clear up in this book. Generally, the length of the Life line does *not* show the length of the life in years, but it *does* represent a factor which well might *influence* just how long a person might live. Let us be more specific.

To begin, we must explain how the date of a person's death is chosen by his guides from the higher planes. When a soul comes into incarnation in a new body, there is selected a period of time when transition out of earth life will take place. However, as the life progresses, it is probable that the person, through his own free-will choices, will shift away from the expected pattern sufficiently to cause the guides to re-assess the most 'beneficial' time of death. They may wish to move that date ahead or defer it beyond the expected time.

We have referred to the time of death as being the most 'beneficial' from the guide's point of view, and we wish to explain this concept in greater detail.

The exact timing of a person's death must be carefully considered by his guides. This timing can itself be used to teach important lessons. If the wrong timing is used, ground can be lost that was won in the life just ended. Consider this example. Suppose a man has been struggling with his self-image for many lives, and finally in the present one he has managed to correct his self-picture to a great degree, through dint of hard effort on his part, and certain confidence-promoting patterns which this life has contained. Then, imagine that the man is driving his car and makes a terrible blunder, deciding to pass the automobile in front when he cannot see sufficiently far ahead of the car to be sure that the roadway is clear. A truck, unseen by our subject, is in a position to collide head-on with the man's car if he proceeds to pass. Now, the guides know how destructive it is for any soul to perceive that it has lost its physical body through stupidity, and they also know that the progress which this man has so recently made could be wiped out in a trice if the accident should happen and be fatal.

These higher entities have access to extra amounts of energy in cases of emergency, and should the man begin to pass the car ahead, they may decide to step in and protect him from his own folly. They have several options: a) they could allow the accident to begin, and then manipulate the space of the three-dimensional world so as to remove his physical body through a fourth-dimensional 'warp' and place it back into the scene some distance away from the wreckage – but still alive. They would have to permit some damage to occur to the body, so as not to raise suspicions that an outside force had come into play – lacerations or a few broken bones would suffice. b) The second option is to take over the man's consciousness for a few moments as he begins to pull ahead to pass, during which time the guides would countermand the decision, and cause the car to pull back. To the man, it would seem as if *he* had made the decision, since the guides would have simply blended their consciousness with his for this brief period. Another option would involve literally removing either the truck or the man's car from the three-dimensional space structure for the time during which contact would have taken place. Then, the vehicle would be placed back into space where it would have been without interference.

The guides usually select the option which requires the least amount of energy to be expended. In the case described, that would have been the second option, in which they manipulate the mind of the driver. In some cases, it is better for the sake of the person they are protecting to select an option which requires more energy. This decision is always carefully weighed.

It might be wondered how the guides are able to know in sufficient time about potential accidents of this kind, and how they can take the time to look at all the options and make the decision before the man obliterates himself on the grill of the truck. To explain this we must first of all point out that each soul in incarnation is watched carefully at all times – not necessarily by his own guide or guardian, but certainly by others who are not so 'high' in their advancement. For example, a watcher could well be a human soul who has recently progressed beyond the necessity for further incarnations on the physical plane, but who has not yet gained sufficient experience or knowledge to be able to directly advise guardians who are faced with decisions of this kind. Such human souls are first taught how to go to and maintain themselves in any realm of the lower worlds, without being subjected to the negativity of that location. Then they are given particular 'watchdog' duties of the kind we have now described. Whenever such a watcher suspects that a dangerous circumstance is about to arise for the individual he is watching, he will immediately signal that to the person's guardian, who will consult with other beings that act as guides for one or more incarnated souls before making a decision as to what, if anything, to do.

We have been using the terms guardian and guide, and we wish to explain clearly what these refer to.

The guardian, as we use the term, is the guardian *angel* – i.e. not a human soul – who has current charge of the particular individual who is incarnated on the earth. The guides with whom the guardian consults are in most cases human souls who have passed beyond the necessity for rebirth. There are numerous exceptions, however, as when a guardian requires specific technical advice and such advice can only come from someone not yet beyond the rebirth cycle.

The 'watcher' as we have called him is going through a kind of training period which eventually will place him among the guides we have now described.

We would like to offer a few more examples relating to the manipulation and selection of an individual's date of death. Firstly we will remind the reader again that only in rare instances is it possible to foresee and to set the death date precisely at the time of birth. Although a general period for death is earmarked, this period will usually change several times during the course of the life. Thus, if a person gives up eating meat, it is necessary for the guides to put off the death date, due to the fact that the karma arising from the eating of flesh will not be so heavy as expected. Or again, if a person takes up the spiritual path and begins to become a beacon of light and truth for his brothers, the guides may well decide to extend the length of life, in view of the possibility that the longer he lives, the more souls will be helped along their paths. Another example relates to a person who is seen to be backsliding, perhaps having fallen in with unsavory companions or having adopted a lifestyle which through drink or drugs or any other physical excess is gradually drawing that person into the downward spiral. The guides and guardians never wish to see any individual lose the gains he has made in this or in previous lives. If necessary, they will seriously consider cutting the life short before irreparable damage is done to the soul's status. Another reason to take an individual out of earth incarnation earlier than previously foreseen is because a perfect opportunity for reincarnation is coming up shortly, and the soul must be in the between-life state in order to qualify for that body. (Occasionally a new body will be 'started' for an individual while he is still living in the old body, and even more rarely the new body will actually be born before the death of the old one. However in the latter case, death of the previous body must take place within a few months of the new birth, since it is too difficult for the soul to deal with two projections at the same time when these projections are not genetically identical.)

Again we have been guilty of digressing rather far away from the subject at hand: palmistry. But we did not wish to lose the opportunity of explaining the process of death-date selection to the reader, since this is pivotal to understanding just what the length of the Life line means.

To return to the Life line, we would point out that the length of the line represents the *originally selected length of the life*, though only at a rough approximation. Moreover, when the foreseen life pattern includes one or several episodes which could *become* the death date, then these times are shown on the Life line as breaks, crossing-lines or faint regions. This brings up a further point that requires elaboration, namely that the guides can often foresee several possible dates for death at the time when the Life line is designed. When this occurs, then the Life line is arranged to show these possibilities in the manner we have indicated.

Another point of importance relates to the comparison between the Life lines on both hands. The guides will often use the writing hand to show the foremost likelihood in terms of length of the life, and the non-writing hand to show the second probability. Additional selections are designated by the breaks, etc we have described.

As to judging the timing of events on the Life line, including the age represented by its termination, the standard scale set out in most of the basic texts on palmistry can be considered correct. The life itself progresses from between the thumb and forefinger downwardly around the ball of the thumb toward the wrist. The half-way point is roughly at age 35.

There are only a few specific points which we wish to make about the Life line beyond the explanation already given, and they are listed below.

• Every line which touches the Life line and which arises on the Mount of Venus (the ball of the thumb) has a *karmic* connotation of some kind. Usually these lines are bunched toward the beginning of the Life line, and if so then they represent the many illnesses of childhood and youth. See Figure 38.

• A line which cuts across the Life line and which also touches the Heart line or the Head line or both, will designate an event or circumstance which involves one or both of the other two facets of the 'triangle' in man. Thus, a line touching Head *and* Life will point to something — not necessarily an illness — which had a *mental* as well as a physical impact. For example it could have been the death of someone close, which caused much stress mentally, and which also caused a debilitation of the physical body. See Figure 39.

• A fainter line which branches out from the Life line and then runs along parallel to the Life line for some distance always designates a *chronic* problem affecting the physical body in some way, for the length of time corresponding to the distance over which the chronic line runs parallel to the Life line.

• A star on the Life line (Figure 40) usually designates the possibility of some traumatic event occurring to the physical body at the age designated by its position. (Likewise, a star on any major line designates a trauma affecting that part of the triangle.)

• A fork in the Life line generally points to a major choice in life's path which must be made at or about the age designated by the fork. It is rarely possible to foresee just what that choice may relate to, without the operation of intuitional or psychic powers.

• A gap in the life line, when bridged by another line which runs parallel and overlaps both the ends (Figure 41) indicates a protective influence operating during the high-risk period designated by the gap.

The Fate Line

The Fate line can be distinguished from other lines on the hand by simply testing to see which line most obviously points toward the Saturn (middle) finger. In any given hand, there will be at least one line that clearly points to Saturn, even though that line may be quite short. The longest of such Saturn-pointing lines should be taken as

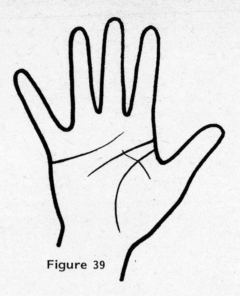

Figure 39

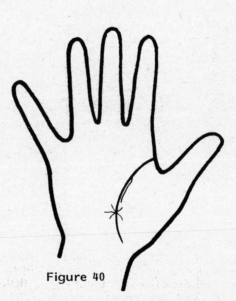

Figure 40

the principal fate line. The Fate line shows primarily the degree of importance which the individual attaches to projecting some image of himself, or 'making his mark in the world'. Those who care little for worldly or career-oriented achievement often have only short Fate lines. Yet others, while not pushing themselves out into the world can be found with long Fate lines. The secret here is to understand that the Fate line does not refer only to *worldly* success. Any individual who has a preconceived picture of his *role* and who actively seeks to *live that role*, will be found to have a discernible fate line. But the role may be that of a housewife and mother. Or again the role may be that of successful businessman. It is possible that both such people could have equally long fate lines. The length of the line tells for what proportion of the life the role is important to that individual. The person who becomes interested in projecting a particular role only after age 30 will have a Fate line which is seen to begin at about the Head line (which marks age 30 on the Fate line, give or take two years). Conversely, the person who projects a role very early in life, but who acquires a philosophy at age 30 which allows him to give up his attachment to his role, and simply take on whatever life offers, will be found to have a fate line which begins near the wrist but which fades out at or about the crossing with the Head line. The *Heart* line crossing on the Fate line represents about age 45.

The general rules which we have set out above also apply to the Fate line, *mutatis mutandis*. Breaks or stars show traumatic events. Branching shows a choice, or more often, the projecting of two roles at once for the length of time that the branches continue together. Figure 41 shows a fate line that speaks of an early projected role in life that was supplemented by a secondary role at about age 25, the first one ceasing around age 29 with the second one continuing.

The Health Line
In Figure 42 the Health line can be seen to begin at about the lower middle of the hand and to extend in the general direction of Mercury (the little finger). That is in fact the way to distinguish be-

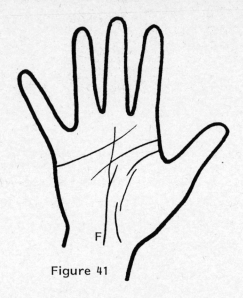

Figure 41

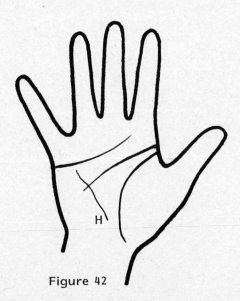

Figure 42

tween more than one possible candidate for the
Health line.

We must first of all stress that *the best Health
line is no Health line at all*. If one must have a
Health line, then the best line is one that goes clean
and straight toward the little finger, with no breaks,
stars or irregularities. Each of the latter markings
represents some episode associated with the general
condition or health of the physical body. Stars
are often, though not always, operations. Breaks
or faint regions in an otherwise clearly marked
Health line can denote times of weakness. However,
do not confuse these with a *general* fading away of
the Health line, for such fading away actually represents an *improvement* in the health picture at the
time indicated.

In the Health line, as in all the longitudinal lines,
any shift in direction or placement which is *toward
the percussion* represents an improvement. In the
Fate line a shift toward the percussion (toward the
Mount of Luna) represents a greater degree of inner
contentment with the direction which the role in life
has taken. This may not correspond with *financial*
improvement.

We do not wish to take further time with this discussion of palmistry. We have provided the main
pointers that will allow the diligent student to push
his knowledge as far as he has time for. We recommend that the student of palmistry obtain and carefully peruse as many texts on the subject as possible. Bear in mind that each is written from that
author's own point of view, and if you come upon a
teaching that does not 'sit right' with you, pass it
over and go on to glean whatever may strike you as
valid from the book. Remember that the subject
was meant to be reasonable to the logical mind, that
the guides have no wish to confuse you, and that,
wherever possible, the most likely correct interpretation will be one that uses the words which qualify
the appearance of the mark and applies them directly to the individual whose hand is being read.

Above all, let the *hands of your brothers* be your
teachers of palmistry. If you will approach the subject with humility, and with an earnest desire to
be of service to humanity through the knowledge
you are seeking, then you may be sure that the
higher entities will take the necessary steps to

bring you the answers you require.

At first, make no statements, but simply ask questions of those willing to let you examine their palms. We repeat, the best teacher of palmistry is the careful examination of actual hands and the posing of questions to those whose palms you study.

Chapter 11

The Head

Having now completed our remarks in regard to
the subject of Palmistry, it remains but to comment
on the symbology relating to the features of the
human head. We have, in our other books, dealt
at some length with the individual significance of
the teeth, the meaning of various nose shapes, the
ear and the eye. However we have not yet explained in a broad sense the whole reason why the human
being *has* a body form which includes a head – a
special anatomical region where the main sensory
pick-ups are located, along with the master control
circuit known as the brain.

To bring this explanation home, it will be necessary for us to point out that such a body form –
one which includes a head – is not the only one
utilized in the cosmos. Even on the earth, where
the 'head-body' form is widely employed among all
animal species, there are some exceptions. Think
of the simpler life-forms like the amoeba. Or again,
there were certain species of dinosaur which were so
large and had so great a tail that a separate 'brain'
was located near the bottom of the spine, just to
handle the tail end of the animal.

Why is it that man recoils from the thought of a
'headless' individual? There is a strange hideous-
ness in the image of the 'Headless Horseman' in the
well-known legend, or in the drinking song which
speaks of the queen with her 'head tucked under-
neath her arm'. Yet why does the thought of some-

one missing an arm or a leg not produce the same
discomfort?

It is simply because every soul incarnate upon the
earth knows that it is through the *head* that the
main connection between the body and the inhabiting
soul arises. It is true that the heart center too is
important as a junction between the lower and the
higher, but the divine spark from the mind of God
dwells in the center of the head, directly beneath
the crown chakra, and indeed it is this fragment of
divinity which gives to that chakra its great power
and light.

When one imagines a person without a head, the
inner knowledge sees a body with no connection to
a higher plane – a robot available for any demonic
influence to control. And indeed, a person who
has 'lost his mind' and become insane is almost always in the grip of some form of unevolved entity.
The entity is not always one of the Dark Brothers,
however, and can be merely a mischievous spirit
seeking some vehicle for influencing, however mar-
ginally, the course of events on earth.

Moreover, when the head is missing, so are the
eyes – which are the portals through which the
soul literally looks out upon the earth plane. Without a head, and without eyes, there is no way to
see the evidence that a soul is in possession of the
body. And this notion is deeply disturbing to any
human within the cycle of rebirth.

We have mentioned the possibility of organizing a
life-form without using a head, and this is done on
some planets where it is not necessary to group the
sensory organs together in one place and where the
body is inhabited by spiritual 'stuff' which is gather-
ed together only for the duration of that body's
existence. This can be compared to the plants and
trees of the earth, in which the indwelling spirit is
not a permanently focused soul or entity as is the
case with human beings. Because the plants and
trees do not require sensory organs, and because
the *entire* spirit of the organism is within it during
its active phase (as contrasted with the human being,
for which only a part of the soul's consciousness
is involved), there is no need for a head as such.
Lest the point we have made be unclear, we will
point out that the plants, flowers and trees act as
'bodies' for spiritual inhabitants which are assem-

bled at the time of germination, and which dissolve
back into the 'Sea of Spirit' when the organism dies,
is eaten or is destroyed. As explained on our book,
Other Kingdoms, the entities responsible for assem-
bling the 'packets' of spiritual stuff to inhabit the
plant or tree are devas – organized beings at a
higher vibration than the physical, which have been
created and trained to carry out these duties. They
select the material to inhabit the germinating plant
or tree on the basis of the vibration or evolvement
of the material (here we mean spiritual material).

Let us turn now to the major features of the head
of the human being. In our earlier books we have
already pointed out the major meanings to be attached to particular shapes of ear, nose, mouth and so
forth. We have requested this channel to provide,
as an appendix to this book, an index of the loca-
tions in the earlier writings where this specific
material can be found. This avoids the necessity of
having to repeat here all of the material which has
already been transmitted. We should point out that
duplication and repetition through a channel is something that is always avoided if possible. In this
book, for the sake of continuity, we have had to
repeat certain concepts which we have explained
elsewhere. However this runs counter to the rule
of efficiency, as we might term it, according to
which a channel should not repeat itself unless necessary, and no channel should comment on the
validity of material being passed through another
channel. This latter rule arises through the desir-
ability of requiring listeners – souls still in incarnation – to look to their own inner guidance when as-
sessing the truth or otherwise of any channel. If
a person could obtain endless commentary from one
channel as to the veracity or accuracy of another,
then he would be tempted to hunt and hunt for such
corroborating testimony *from outside himself*, and he
would never be brought to see that the only true
measuring stick for him is the quiet knowledge of
truth within his own heart's center.

The Chin

This portion of the facial anatomy is directly linked to the aggressive energies – those which respond
to the planet Mars. A cleft shows that any aggressiveness which may be present arises through a

failure thus far to reconcile the warring male and
female sides of the individual. A tendency to suppress one and elevate the other aggravates the aggressive urges. Typically the cleft is found in men,
and the result is a tendency to allow the aggressive
traits to surface against the spouse.

Marks, warts, scars and the like all point to particular energy complexes relating to aggression which
have been collected in past lives and which must
be worked out or dealt with in the present life.

The Mouth

The technique of reading the course of the life
along the lips from right to left has already been
explained in our earlier writings. A cleft in the
lips, usually the upper lip, again points to unresolved hostility in the male/female equation of the
soul. However, in the case of the cleft palate, the
unresolved inner conflict has in past lives led the
soul to practice continued cruelty against the spouse,
for which the karma is to endure a life with this dis-
figuration.

The Teeth

Each tooth has a well-defined meaning in terms
of the traits of the individual, and the reader
is directed to our other writings for a detailed
analysis.

When one has a separation between the two upper
front teeth (equivalent to a cleft), the significance
is again that there remains some unresolved conflict
between the male and female parts of the soul. However the result of the conflict is to impell the individual in the direction of worldly success, however he
may define this. There is a tendency to place such
success well ahead of other, more human values and
pleasures. As a result, if pushed too far, this
trait will often bring sorrow into the personal life –
as a form of lesson for the individual.

The Cheeks

These parts of the facial anatomy pertain to the
sexual lessons in a general way. Evident birthmarks
or warts on the cheeks relate almost always to past
life episodes in which the person was guilty of having forced sexual attentions upon another against
the other's will. In consequence, the person in the

present life would normally have to undergo experiences in which the tables were turned, and the same embarrassment and humiliation were experienced.

The Nose
We have dealt with the nose too in our earlier books. Here we wish to point out the meaning of a *cleft* in the nose. As will be suspected by the reader, the cleft — wherever it appears — always betokens some unresolved conflict or hostility between the male and female sides of the soul, which is adversely affecting the course of the life pattern in some way. The nose represents the self-image, and any noticeable cleft in this part indicates that the self-image is poor or inadequate in some way *due to this inner conflict*. For example, the individual may desperately wish not to appear to have any of the characteristics of the opposite sex. If a man, he would have perhaps an inordinate fear of appearing effeminate in some way. A female (for females this mark is quite rare) might strive to suppress her natural 'masculine' traits of adventurousness, or aggression, or desire for success in the world's eyes. The result of this struggle is seriously to impair the self-picture, and as a consequence, the life is filled with trial and inner strain.

The Upper Lip
In addition to the meaning of this portion in terms of the course of the mental life (see Appendix), there is a further significance: it is that of haughtiness, the assumption that one is superior to others. When there occurs a mark, wart or scar on the upper life, it will have meaning not only in terms of the course of the mental life-experiences, but will also point to a karmic necessity to endure a period of subservience or low position in society or work, in order to erase from the soul any lingering haughtiness or superiority complex which was erected in a past life or lives.

The Brow
The 'Mark of Cain', originally applied to Adam's son because he had murdered Abel, consists of four roughly vertical lines which seem to pass through the eyes — two on each side, as in Figure 43. When

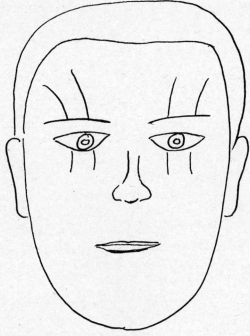

Figure 43

this is found, the meaning is more complex than merely that of murder. We wish to emphasize that there is hardly a soul now incarnate upon the earth who has not been responsible for the death of at least one other soul in some prior life. Thus to have been an agent of death for another is not specifically what the Mark of Cain betokens. Its meaning is that the karma arising from the murders that were committed in past lives *has not yet been fully set aside*.

It is important to understand, in this connection, that there is more than one way to set aside karma relating to murder. Indeed, if the only way to meet such karma were to die in a similar situation, then there are many individuals who simply would not have sufficient lives to be able to set all their karma aside. Many souls have been directly responsible for the deaths of hundreds, even thousands, and yet the number of lives allotted to each soul is only in the area of 50 or so (the number varies, depending upon several complex factors).

One way of setting aside death-related karma is to *give birth*. Indeed, the birth labour undergone by a woman is also used to allow her to meet any pain-related karma arising from the death which is being set aside by the new life being brought forth. Hence the pain of labour.

Another way to meet such karma is to serve the race in a spiritual sense. To rescue a soul from the obliteration of the downward spiral more than compensates for having taken a physical body from a soul through murder. Indeed, many individuals who have dedicated themselves to spiritual work – almost to the point of fanaticism – are ones who know deep within that they must find a way to offset the death and destruction for which they once were responsible.

Thus, those who have the four-fold mark on the brow would do well to begin to seek a higher path, if they are not already living a spiritually aware life. Moreover, the individual vertical lines each refer to some basic flaw in the soul's make-up that stands in need of correction in this life. The lines passing through the right eye pertain to some problem connected with the male side of the soul, while those on the left relate to the female side. The specific meaning however, can only be determined through a detailed analysis of other signals on the

body, and from a thorough knowledge of the temper-
ament of the individual.

A *cleft* in the brow between the eyes again points
to an unresolved conflict between the male and female sides of the soul. In this case, the conflict
has resulted in some over-emphasis in connection
with the sexual nature. This lopsidedness is not
always in the direction of sexual obsession, but
can be the reverse of that. The main point is that
a conflict in the male/female pattern of the soul is
producing some strain in the life due to a lopsidedness in connection with sexuality.

The Ears

We have dealt with the ears at length in our other
writings. Here we would simply point out that a
cleft in the ear *lobe*, seen usually as a diagonal line
running through the lobe, shows that the unresolved
male/female conflict at the soul level is producing
physical problems, usually in relation to the abdominal organs. Medical science has associated this
signal with diabetes, and it is true that many dia-
betics have such a line. However, the presence of
this mark can also betoken digestive difficulties,
liver problems, and other afflictions relating to the
abdominal organs.

The Eye

At last we come to what is, in many respects, the
most important and most revealing part of the entire
body – for it is through the eyes that we discover
the true inner essence of any person. The soul
knows that its real nature is laid bare to one who
looks it directly in the eyes, and for this reason
there are many who avoid the glance of others. They
do not wish the other person to see the stains which
are on the soul, so they shut the portals through
which the blemish is visible.

If ever you wish to see what any person is truly
like, then simply study his eyes. There you can
read honesty or criminality, worldliness or spiritual
striving, kindness or cruelty, gentleness or aggression. The eyes of one who has progressed far along
his quest for God are vastly different from the eyes
of him who knows not that he is a spiritual being.

Eyes may open wide, or may shut to small slits.
Here is the signal which tells how open and forth-

coming is the soul. He who closes the eyes to a mere slit is shuting himself away from others — through distrust, anger or the memory of an ancient pain in another life. There are eyes that speak of kindness and a gentle heart, to whom the weary in soul turn for solace. There are eyes that know truth with a deep and burning certitude, and to these come the seekers of the world. And there are eyes that have seen the Countenance of God with a pure heart — and these are the eyes of the great Way-Showers of all the ages.

Seekers of the Light: Remember that your eyes, your hearts, your bodies — are the instruments that God uses to rescue His other children from their own folly. Remember too that on each of His children the Creator of All That Is has placed the sure signs of identity — which tell the truth to any with eyes to see. Your feet are inscribed with a microcosm of your physical form; your legs represent the lower and higher selves and remind you always to bring these into alignment; your internal organs relate to facets of the higher self and reflect in their debilities the work and learning that yet must be attended to; the palms and fingers of your hands are a beautiful map on which you can trace the course of your life, and the outworking of the multicolored facets of your soul; and your eyes are the portals of the divine part of you — through which your soul looks out upon God's creation, and through which your brothers can commune directly with your true essence.

May you ever be mindful of the sacredness of the temple which you inhabit. It is a gift from the Creator, who has minutely marked it with all of the information you require to allow you to steer your passage safely among the rocks and shoals of reality.
Remember where you are going.
And look to the signs on your physical form to remind you where you have been.

May the peace and blessing of all the higher beings who care for humanity's struggle be with you forevermore.

OM MANI PADME HUM

The appendix which follows contains an alphabetical listing of all references in the Hilarion Series of books, including Lightline (Newsletter), which pertain to the symbology and meaning of the body and its diseases. References are made using two-letter codes for the various books in the series, as follows:

NR   Nature of Reality
SS   Seasons of the Spirit
SY   Symbols
TH   Threshold
IG   The Inert Gases
OK   Other Kingdoms

For the references to Lightline, the issue number is designated along with the page number. Double and triple issues are identified by the first number of the composite issue. Thus, LL/1/7 means Lightline 1,2,3 (composite issue), page 7. LL/19/10 simply means page 10 of Lightline No. 19 (single issue). For the books, the page number is given after the slash ("/").